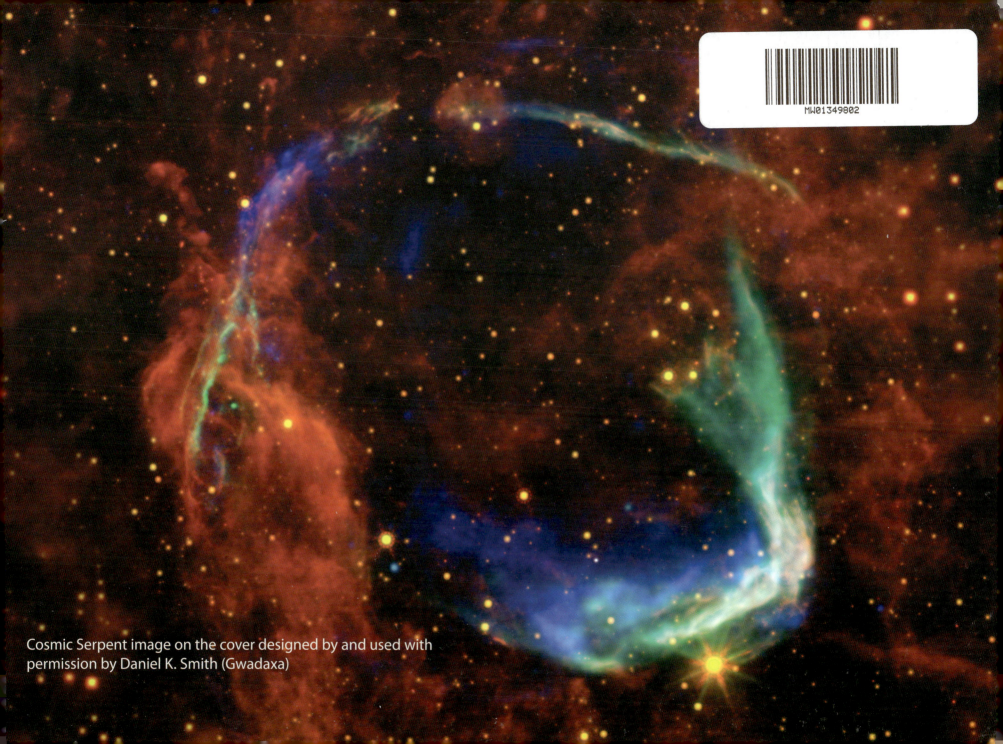

Cosmic Serpent image on the cover designed by and used with permission by Daniel K. Smith (Gwadaxa)

Nā Koa Moʻo

Native Hawaiian Warrior Chant written for the Cosmic Serpent Project

He mai, he heahea, he ohooho!
A call, a welcome, an acclaimation!

E nā moo o ka lewa lani, nā moo o ke kai uli
nā moo o ke ao, nā moo o ka pō
nā moo o ka pāpapa, nā moo o ke kualono
nā moo o nā mokuhonua, nā moo o nā mokupuni
nā moo o ka wao one, nā moo o ka ōnaeao ē
Oh serpents of the multiple heavens, of the deep sea
of the dark of night, of the light of day,
of the shoals and reefs, of the mountain ridges
of the continents, of the islands
of the deserts and plains, oh serpents of the universe

E hō mai ka ike, e hō mai ka mana, e hō mai ke aloha ē
I hā, i eaea, i ola loa nō ē
E nenee mai, e pili mai,
E kōkua mai i ou mau koa, i ou mau keiki
Grant us knowledge, grant us strength, grant us love
Breath into us life, a long life indeed
Move close, cleave to us,
Give aid to your warriors, to your children

Imua e nā koa o ka mauli ola, i ola mau nā loina o nā kūpuna
i ka wai ike, i ka wai puna, i ka wai ola, e kena ai ka puu ē
Forward, warriors of Indigenous essence so the customs of our
ancestors will live in the waters of knowledge and life our thirst will
be quenched

Kaimanaonālani Barcarse

E ola nā moo, he moolelo, he mookūpuna, he mookiina
he mooakua, o ka moolewalipo ē
Life to the serpents, the story, the genealogy, the processes,
the godly ceremonies, indeed life to the cosmic serpent!

E lele, e kolo, e au, e pii, e holo, e kaua no ka pono ōiwi
Fly, crawl, swim, climb, run, go forth and fight for our Native ways

na D.N. Kaimanaonālani Barcarse
24-25.I.2011, Ma ke kulu aumoe,
me ke kā a Makalii ma ka lolopua

The Cosmic Serpent

Bridging Native Ways of Knowing and Western Science in Museum Settings.

A Collaboration between the Indigenous Education Institute and the
University of California, Berkeley's Center for Science Education at the Space Sciences Laboratory,
funded by the National Science Foundation.

Authors: Nancy C. Maryboy, Ph.D., David Begay, Ph.D., Laura Peticolas, Ph.D.

Evaluator Authors: Jill Stein and Shelly Valdez, Ph.D.

Editor / Layout / Graphic Design: Christopher S. Teren

Editing: Karin Hauck, Ruth Paglierani, and Renee Frappier

Graphic Design: Ashley C. Teren

National Science Foundation Grant
DRL-0714631 & DRL-0714629

Copyright 2012
Indigenous Education Institute

Dedication:

In memory of Angayuqaq Oscar Kawagley, Ph.D. (1934-2011) who contributed so much to our path of knowing.

"...The cry of the raven is encouraging us to balance our physical, emotional, intellectual, and spiritual selves, and to walk peacefully as we extend our ways to others and in our own Native languages."

Piurciqukut yuluta pitaliketuluta -
"We will become people living a life that feels just right.

Quyana!"

Acknowledgement and gratitude to Angayuqaq Oscar Kawagley and Ray Barnhardt who have demonstrated and lived collaboration with integrity.

"The depth of Indigenous knowledge rooted in the long inhabitation of a particular place offers lessons that can benefit everyone, from educator to scientist, as we search for a more satisfying and sustainable way to live on this planet."

—Angayuqaq Oscar Kawagley, Ph.D. and Ray Barnhardt, Ph.D.

Table of Contents

East: Ha'a'aah – Place of Initiation (Nitsáhákees)

Section 1: The Cosmic Serpent: A Global Archetype	14
Section 2: The Diné Cosmic Model	16
Section 3: Gaining Awareness of Worldviews	18
Section 4: Similarities with Western Science	26

South: Shádi'ááh – Place of Organization & Growth (Nahat'á)

Section 5: Building Relationships	30
Section 6: Developing the Process	20
Section 7: Pilot Workshop	22
Section 8: Restructure Workshops	24

West: I'i'aah – Process of Activation – Living It... (Íí'ná)

Section 9: Southwest Workshops	26
Section 10: Northwest Workshops	30
Section 11: California Workshops	36
Section 12: Culminating Conference	42

North: Náhookos – Process of Transformation and Renewal (Siihasin)

Section 13: Transformation	50
Section 14: Renewal	56
Section 15: Evaluation / Outcomes	58
Section 16: Sustainability	60

Resources

Advisors	95
Cosmic Serpent Fellows	96
Participating Institutions	98

Contributors

People who contributed to this book	100
Cosmic Serpent Team Leadership	101
Refrences and Resources	103

Credits

Photographs, Illustrations	108

Acknowledgments

A Special Thank You To...	109

The Cosmic Serpent Project's website can be found at http://cosmicserpent.org

Diné Cosmic Model Table of Contents - Process Model

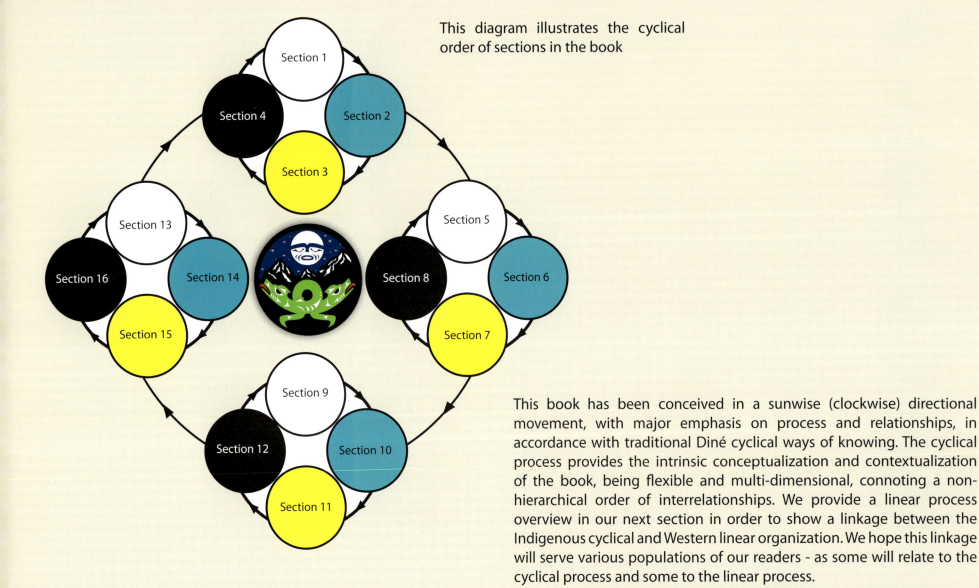

This diagram illustrates the cyclical order of sections in the book

This book has been conceived in a sunwise (clockwise) directional movement, with major emphasis on process and relationships, in accordance with traditional Diné cyclical ways of knowing. The cyclical process provides the intrinsic conceptualization and contextualization of the book, being flexible and multi-dimensional, connoting a non-hierarchical order of interrelationships. We provide a linear process overview in our next section in order to show a linkage between the Indigenous cyclical and Western linear organization. We hope this linkage will serve various populations of our readers - as some will relate to the cyclical process and some to the linear process.

Diné Cosmic Model Table of Contents – Process Model with Section Titles

This diagram illustrates the inter-relationships of section titles in the book.

The sun-like symbol illustrates an igniting force, which begins the process. In this book, the igniter is the introduction... Igniting the spark.

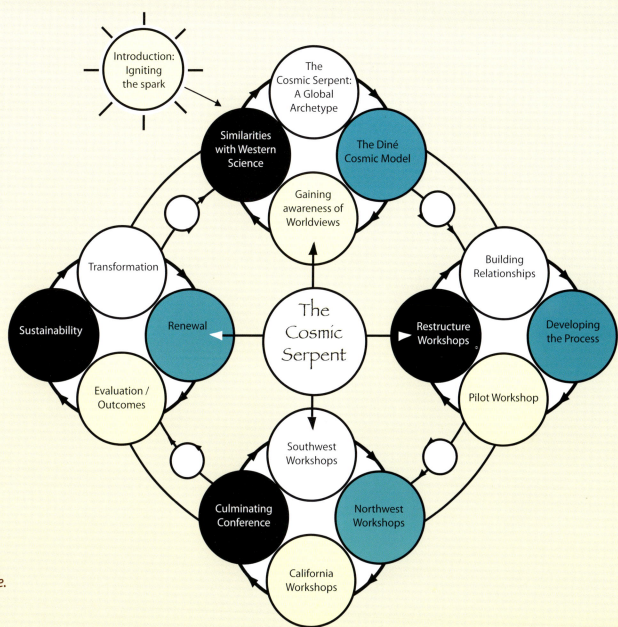

Models courtesy of Indigenous Education Institute.
Maryboy / Begay 2011

Introduction: Igniting the Spark – Who, Why and Wherefore

Setting the Stage

This book is a deliverable (requisite) of an NSF (National Science Foundation) grant to share the project outcomes and what we learned from the NSF grant project. This four-year NSF project was funded to provide professional development to museum educators about Indigenous Knowledge and Western Science in museums, with the goal of providing a culturally relevant way for Indigenous communities to connect to science. The name of this grant was "Cosmic Serpent: Bridging Native Ways of Knowing and Western Science in Museum Settings." This book is also a snapshot in time of this work in Indigenous Knowledge and Western Science in museums. That is, this book is a written document that describes our understandings of these science education concepts today, built on work done in the past, and constantly evolving with continued research into the future. It is within this context that we provide a bit of history of how this NSF project came to be.

The seed for this work was planted, so-to-speak, many years ago with the collaboration between an astronomer/science educator at UCB (University of California, Berkeley), Dr. Isabel Hawkins, and a Cherokee-Navajo astronomer/science educator from IEI (Indigenous Education Institute), Dr. Nancy Maryboy. After years of working together, and with others, around the ideas of cultural relevance of science to Indigenous communities, they began to work to obtain NSF funding to develop professional development workshops for informal educators to sustain the work they had begun. One book that inspired Nancy and Isabel at this stage was "Cosmic Serpent" by Jeremy Narby. Dr. David Begay, Navajo astronomer/science educator at IEI, joined the team to develop the proposal for the project. Isabel, Nancy, and David then collaborated with Dr. Mary Marcussen (Marcussen & Associates) to help focus the envisioned project on the most important science education research and best practices in the ISE (Informal Science Education) field. The ISE field is in the field of study that understands how we learn outside of the classroom.

Ms. Ruth Paglierani, science educator at UCB, also joined the team, with a wealth of experience envisioning and implementing science education programs. David and Nancy had worked for years with their own Cherokee and Navajo (Diné) communities in science and science education. Ruth and Isabel had collaborated for years on science education work around the world. The collaboration between Nancy, David, Isabel, and Ruth made for a strong and robust partnership that had been built over time. Throughout the proposal process and the project itself, our program officer at NSF (National Science Foundation), Dr. Sylvia James, helped the Cosmic Serpent team to understand the goals of NSF and how this project could support those goals.

The collaborative project was funded in 2007 with Dr. Nancy Maryboy as overall PI (Principal Investigator). Dr. Isabel Hawkins and Dr. David Begay were Co-Principal Investigators (Co-PIs) and Ruth Paglierani was Project Manager. Dr. Martin Storksdieck was the lead evaluator of the project from ILI (Institute for Learning Innovation), and together with Jill Stein, also of ILI, and Dr. Shelly Valdez, of Native Pathways, made up the evaluation team. Wendy Pollock was the education partner from the ASTC (Association for Science and Technology Centers) and Pam Woodis was the education partner from the NMAI (National Museum of the American Indian).

After the work was funded, the partnerships that developed during the writing of the proposal continued, but several specific individuals moved to other things, while other individuals joined the team. In the second year of the project (2008), Isabel retired from her position at UCB. Dr. Laura Peticolas, space scientist and educator, who had worked in Isabel's group for five years and had collaborated with Isabel on many projects, took over Isabel's role as Co-Lead on Cosmic Serpent. Laura had never before worked with Nancy and David. While working to accomplish the goals of the project, it took about a year to develop a strong collaboration with solid communication between this new leadership. Renee Frappier, at UCB, took on the role as project manager with Ruth supporting the leadership team in design of the professional development workshops. Ashley Teren came on board as project manager with IEI. Around this same time, Dr. Martin Storksdieck moved to work at the National Academies of Science on "A Framework for K-12 Science Education: Practices, Crosscutting Concepts, and Core Ideas" (NRC, 2011) Jill Stein and Dr. Shelly Valdez remained as evaluators on the project but took over the evaluation lead as a collaborative team. Dr. Eric Jones joined the evaluation team. Wendy Pollock moved to other projects and Laura Huerta-Migus took on the ASTC - partner role. Over the years of the project, this Cosmic Serpent team became a strong collaboration between all ten individuals who represented six different institutions from science education and Indigenous communities.

A Direct, Explicit, and Linear Explanation of this Book

This book was written in a collaborative manner, modeling the way in which the NSF (National Science Foundation) Cosmic Serpent project was developed and carried out. That is, the book was written with leadership from Dr. Nancy C. Maryboy, Dr. David Begay, and Dr. Laura Peticolas as a collaborative team working closely together. It was written with strong input from Ruth Paglierani, Dr. Isabel Hawkins, Renee Frappier, and Ashley Teren. Jill Stein, Dr. Shelly Valdez, and Dr. Eric Jones provided the voice, not only of the Cosmic Serpent Fellows, the participants of the workshops, but also of Western Evaluation thought (Jill and Eric) and Indigenous Evaluation processes (Shelly). In this book, the Cosmic Serpent Fellows share their views on the project directly through quotes of their own, through the evaluation, and indirectly through conversations with the Cosmic Serpent team. The Cosmic Serpent Fellows are the heart of this project – they are the people who participated in the professional development workshops, bringing their knowledge and perspectives with them and taking back what they learned to their museums. The book also contains the voice of the community of American Indians through Pam Woodis (National Museum of American Indian, NMAI) and Laura Huerta-Migus (Association of Science - Technology Centers, ASTC) who provides the voice of America's science centers and museums. Ashley Teren provided graphics and captions to the photographs. Traci Walter provided support in ensuring we had permission to use the photographs and in gathering the resources and citations. Christopher Teren was the main designer and editor of the layout of the book, and contributed graphics.

Karin Hauck of UCB (University of California, Berkeley) worked with Christopher Teren and the team on editing and layout. Dr. Bryan Mendez (of UCB) and Dr. Mary Marcussen reviewed the initial draft of the book and provided comments. Because this book was written in a collaborative fashion, input from all of these voices are interwoven throughout this book. We further acknowledge with gratitude all who helped to develop and implement this project and the project deliverables towards the 'end' of this book.

The intent of this book is to share our Cosmic Serpent project and highlight significant outcomes. This book has been written for the broadest audience possible.

- For the American public, we hope this book provides valuable information that may inspire all people to learn more about science and how it relates to their own culture;
- For educators who work with science museums, tribal museums, cultural museums and the diversity of the public who visit museums, we hope this book provides valuable lessons from our project on how to collaborate with integrity and connect with Native people, and that it provides ideas for connecting with the diversity of cultures in the United States around science and knowing;

- For Native Americans and other Indigenous people, we hope this book demonstrates how Native Ways of Knowing can be brought with mutual respect to the science community and how science could be a useful tool to enhance Native ways of knowing
- For scientists, we hope this project provides an awareness of Indigenous ways of knowing and guidance to those who would like to collaborate with Indigenous Knowledge holders to better understand the complexity and interrelationships of the world and universe in which we live.

We attempted to create a book that was not limited to a particular sector of the public, with as little text as possible and as many images and photographs as possible. We hope that this book is both read by the layperson as well as those in the professional informal science education field.

There are many challenges in writing a book such as this. This book was designed and organized to be accessed in at least two different ways. In one way, it can be approached as a cyclical and holistic document, coming back to certain important ideas again and again. This is a complex model whose nature is reflected in its cyclic and fractal nature, as it uses the Diné Cosmic Model as a structure (Maryboy & Begay, 1998). It was written to honor the Cosmic Serpent project model, of having the Indigenous voice lead the project, but allowing access to the work by all readers. This book can also be approached in a linear fashion, with concepts building on one another as they are introduced throughout the book and then, finally, expanding on them on toward the end. In both approaches, we designed the document to be read in its entirety, to be absorbed as a complete work. We imagine readers engaging with it actively and completely, including perhaps even "talking back to it" or "discussing with it". We have found from reviewers, that this book brings up many different emotions and we urge our readers to engage with those emotions and the Cosmic Serpent content as much as possible, as this indicates to us a true learning process.

> *Western Science:* We use this term throughout this book and the Cosmic Serpent project because the cross-cultural collaborations require us to put science into a cultural context. Using "Western Science" instead of "science" is a reminder that what we call science today has its origins in Western, or Eurocentric, cultures. The term Western Science conveys that the science of which we speak includes the Western European cultural ways of understanding nature and the universe. In the Cosmic Serpent project these cultural ways of understanding nature are juxtaposed with Native or Indigenous ways of understanding nature.
>
> *Native Science, Indigenous Knowledge and Native Ways of Knowing:* We use these terms throughout this book, somewhat interchangeably. We often use "ways of knowing", because knowledge can imply a static body of information. "Ways" of knowing reminds us that there is more than one way of knowing. "Knowing" reminds us that our knowledge is a dynamic, ever-moving process. "Native Science" is sometimes used to remind us that the word "science" originates from the concept of knowing.
>
> *For more information on the reasons for using this terminology, please see Maryboy & Begay, 1998 and "Bridging Cultures: Indigenous and Scientific Ways of Knowing Nature" (Aikenhead and Michell, 2011)*

Linear Site-Map of Book

Next we provide a linear "roadmap" to the book for our readers who would like to understand where they might find certain topics or information within the book. We hope this will allow such readers to jump to the section relevant to their own inquiry about this Cosmic Serpent project.

- This introduction starts in 'igniting' the book's cyclical process.
- The main sections of the book are organized according to the Diné Cosmic Model (Maryboy & Begay, 1998). The chapter and section titles of the book are presented in this holistic Diné Cosmic Model circular graphic on pages VIII-IX in order to show the inter-relatedness of every section. If we were not limited by the linear and two-dimensionality of a book, we could perhaps present the connections between sections and ideas more easily. But we have done the best we can within the construct of a book.
- In Chapter "East: Ha'a'aah - Place of Initiation (Nitsáhákees)", we present the beginnings of the project, including 1) the Cosmic Serpent Diné Cosmic Model that includes the project goals and objectives, 2) the reason for the name of this project "Cosmic Serpent", 3) thoughts on the team's collaboration at this early stage of the project and 4) a glimpse into commonalities and differences in Indigenous ways of knowing and scientific process with many references at the end to learn more.
- In Chapter "South: Shádi'ááh - Place of Organization & Growth (Nahat'á)", we present the process by which we began the work to provide professional development workshops to science center, tribal museum, and cultural museum practitioners. We describe our first pilot workshop and the findings from this first workshop. Written documents such as this book are helpful; however we demonstrate and stress the importance of learning this content by way of cross-cultural partnerships that first and foremost require ample time to develop as well as significant face-to-face time.
- In Chapter "West: I'i'aah - Process of Activation - Living It...(Ii'ná)", we present information about the six week-long professional development workshops we hosted during 3 years of the project. As our entire project was built around in-person meetings, we dedicate a large part of this book towards describing the workshops and highlighting different tools and approaches within the agendas, which were especially effective. In these workshops, as with this book, we have emphasized the Indigenous worldview as this is not taught in mainstream culture, whereas science is. We had and have to find the balance between these two worldviews, by spending more time creating awareness of Native ways of knowing.
- In Chapter "North: Náhookos - Process of Transformation and Renewal (Siihasin)", we share out the results of this project in terms of collaborations that took place and public experiences that were created in part due to the Cosmic Serpent workshops. We also present what we have learned from this project both as leaders of the project as well as from our evaluation team. We provide evidence on how sustainability of this work is built into the process of relationship. Through Cosmic Serpent Fellows' partnerships between Cosmic Serpent Fellows, projects at museums involving Western Science and Native Ways of Knowing are just now sprouting up around the Western United States.
- Throughout the document we bring the voices of the Cosmic Serpent Fellows, the participants of our workshops, into this book via actual quotes. The Cosmic Serpent Fellows are the focus of the project and the central driving force that allowed us to create this book. They are the hope and inspiration for the sustainability and dissemination of programs and products that value and present Native Ways of Knowing – the knowledge of nature brought about by observations and data by people and the natural system developed by thousands of years of living in one place – together with the abstracted and generalized knowledge of Western science based on observation and data often collected by sophisticated modern technology.
- In the later pages of the book, we acknowledge all the people who were a part of this project, from our NSF (National Science Foundation) project manager and our grant writer, to our team, the Cosmic Serpent Fellows and their institutions, and our advisors and presenters. Hundreds of people took part in this project and it was only because of so many people's dedication that this project succeeded in the way that it did.

Project Overview

The Indigenous Education Institute and the UC Berkeley Space Sciences Laboratory developed Cosmic Serpent, a professional development project, to increase the capacity of museum practitioners to bridge Native and Western science learning in informal settings.

Cosmic Serpent set out to explore commonalities between Western and Native science, taking into account that Native cultures have, over millennia, developed ways of knowing that are highly adapted, interconnected, and enduring. Each knowledge system informs the practice of science and its role in society in a fundamental way, and the commonalities can provide a framework for developing mutually inclusive learning experiences in STEM (science, technology, engineering, and mathematics).

Deliverables included:

- Professional development workshops and peer mentoring
- Museum programs featuring Native/Western commonalities as entry points to STEM
- Regional partnerships among museums and Native communities
- Multimedia resources
- A legacy document to inform the ISE field on ways to improve STEM programming for Native Americans
- A culminating conference jointly hosted by NMAI (National Museum of the American Indian) and ASTC (Association of Science & Technology Centers). The project was guided and sustained by Native and Western scholars experienced in bridging Native ways of knowing and Western science. This book serves as the 'legacy document' mentioned as Deliverable 5.

Cosmic Serpent served 162 practitioners from 41 science centers/museums and 42 tribal/cultural museums and/or communities in the U.S. Southwest, West, and Northwest (eight states). The intended outcomes of the project were to: 1) increase participants' understanding of Native and Western science and awareness of the potentialities of the intersection of the two knowledge systems; 2) develop museum community programs that reflect these commonalities; 3) foster enduring and respectful partnerships between museums and Native communities; and 4) increase institutional capacity to engage Native audiences in science.

Evaluation conducted by the Institute for Learning Innovation and Native Pathways tracked participant outcomes and the potential for broader sustainable impact on their institutions. The project incorporated a new approach toward evaluation, one that embraces joint interpretation of data by teams with different yet complementary evaluation approaches (informal science evaluation and Indigenous evaluation), and that models the type of cross-cultural collaboration that the project itself is designed to support.

Susan Sheopships from Tamástslikt Cultural Institute at the Fairbanks Workshop

East: Ha'a'aah – Place of Initiation
Section 1 … The Cosmic Serpent: A Global Archetype

The Cosmic Serpent is a trans-cultural icon. It is a global symbol that highlights the interconnected nature of fundamental concepts in earth, space, life and environmental sciences.

Around the world, for thousands of years, in one form or another, the reptilian serpent (snake, dragon, Naga - of Hindu tradition, the Native Hawaiian mo'o) has been an archetype for countless tribes, societies and civilizations. In almost every instance, the serpent stands for immense and powerful cosmic movements. This is true of archetypal serpents deep under the earth, deep under the oceans, on the earth surface and in the sky. In fact, it is the very ability of serpents to move between various worlds and different dimensions which give them a significance, providing purpose and direction to ways of knowing and being, world-wide. Other physical and transformational qualities of serpents, such as the shedding of their skins symbolizing regeneration, add to their complex, mutable characteristics, illustrating the awe with which they are regarded.

Indigenous cultures around the world use cultural lore in the form of story to teach important lessons applicable to life. Many of these stories, often termed "myth" have foundational representations of the natural world, including the human connection and human participation in the place in which they live. Sometimes the cosmic serpent is viewed as representative of negative energy, sometimes as positive and sometimes as providing balance and/or ambivalence.

Australian Aboriginal woodcarving.

Double-headed serpents are seen in some of the rock carvings of Pacific Northwest Coast tribes. These carvings are found in specific places where geologists are now finding that massive earthquakes took place. In Guatemala researchers are finding links between traditional serpent stories and large landslides and earthquakes. In Australia, Aboriginal stories from knowledge going back more than 40,000 years, tell of Rainbow serpents guarding pure water holes and underground aquifers, in the world's driest continent.

The Cosmic Serpent archetype as it pervades many different cultures seems to speak to the idea that our diverse cultures have many things in common. As Indigenous scholar Phillip Duran says, "the archetype has a specific meaning within each culture, yet as a global symbol it helps to convey the message that all cultures are interconnected by virtue of their humanity and, more specifically, it conveys what the project hopes to accomplish, which is to build bridges between Western and Native world views."

We have chosen the archetype of the Cosmic Serpent to identify this project. This is truly one symbol that can speak to the interconnections, relationships and processes of many cultures, and is illustrated through centuries of art, music, song, observation, and science.

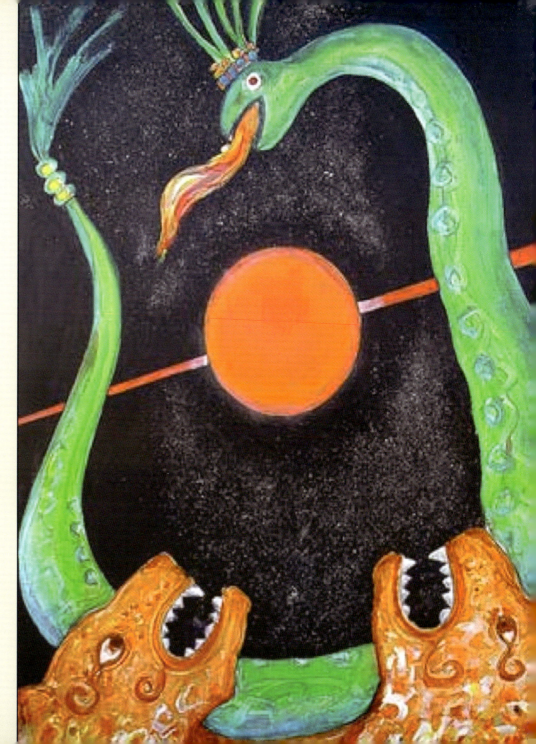

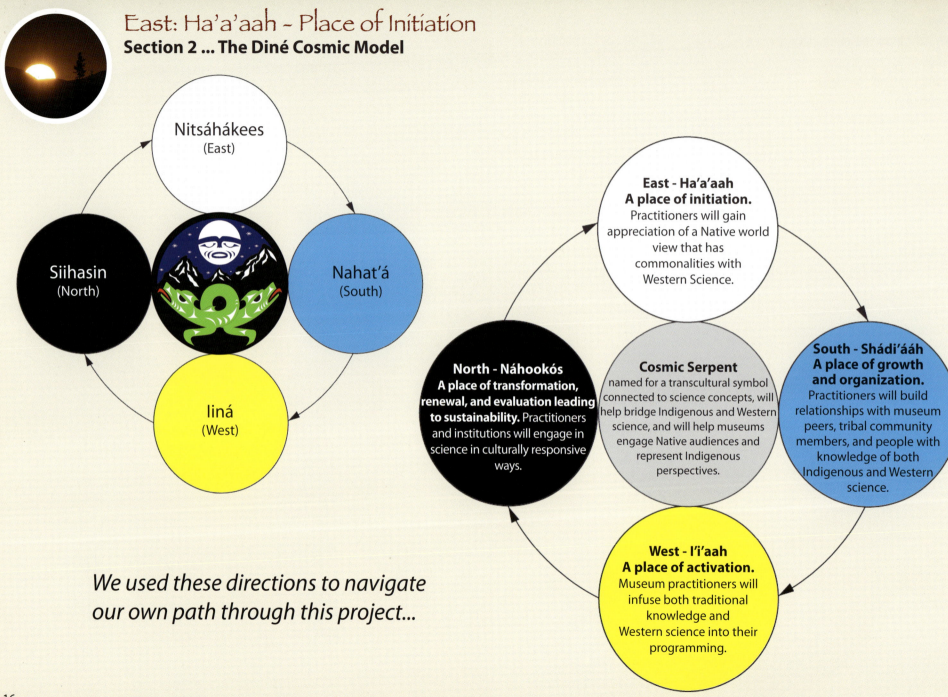

The Cosmic Serpent project used an Indigenous-based strategic planning model to organize itself. The four strategic goals written into the Cosmic Serpent project were based on the tenets and planning principles of this Indigenous-based strategic planning model. This process model was developed from observation of the natural cosmic order, and using the natural processes created by the natural order to provide organization and structure. Relevant strategic planning principles and tenets extracted from the observable natural order were utilized for the planning and evaluation of the Cosmic Serpent project. This planning model was developed from the cultural songs and stories of the Navajo (Diné) that have been shared and passed down for countless generations in the American Southwest. In essence, the model and its processes, organization and structure are replicated from the natural cosmic order. Nature provides the planning model, organization, processes, and structure.

Like nature itself, the model is a cyclical process. For this project, we simplified the process into four quadripartite circles with a central organizing focus. The center, which constantly changes dynamically, provides the organizing process, and ultimately connects all components of the planning process with specified desired outcomes. For example, in this case, one of the central organizing forces becomes the project vision, that in turn drives the entire process with goals, sub-goals, and with ultimate measurable outcomes and evaluations.

This Indigenous-based strategic planning model demands one to start with the end, or desirable outcome, in mind. From the end in mind, we develop the process and means by which to articulate and achieve the end result. Like the natural cosmic order, the model provides processes, order, and structure.

This model is dynamic, and can be adapted to multiple uses depending on unique organizational and planning needs. We have used the four seasons, and four cardinal directions, organized into quadrants, using the four colors of the sky in the natural order as perceived by the Diné people: pre-dawn (white), midday (blue), evening twilight (yellow), darkness (black). The process illustrated in the model moves in a sun-wise (clockwise) direction.

The Diné Cosmic Model (copyright, 1998, 2003, 2007) was developed by David Begay and Nancy C. Maryboy with the Indigenous Education Institute. It has been applied to planning activities with several federal grants and has been used for strategic planning and evaluation by many institutions, nationwide.

The Diné Cosmic Model (DCM) has some relational aspects of other planning models, such as the Logic Model developed and used by the Kellogg Foundation. In the case of the DCM every part of the model, including the most intricate and complex interrelationships, come from nature's own natural order and interrelationship of all things. Nature, as illustrated in the DCM, has the capacity to generate its own order and corrective actions using feedback loops to correct imbalances. The DCM, in collaboration with the evaluation team, has developed a network to ensure concerns are properly addressed and corrected. Names and words carry deep interrelationship meanings, and hold special significance in Indigenous languages, which do not always translate easily into English. Traditional knowledge is place-based, and comes from the land and the location to the sky. The model was conceived in the Navajo language and translated into English.

East: Ha'a'aah - Place of Initiation
Section 3 ... Gaining Awareness of Worldviews

Practitioners will gain appreciation of a Native worldview of science that has commonalities with Western science.

In this place of initiation, the collaboration between the partners IEI (Indigenous Education Institute), UCB (University of California), NMAI (National Museum of the American Indian), and the ASTC (Association of Science and Technology Centers) began in a sense with the Diné Cosmic Model. The model helped keep the team's focus on the goal of the project. It provided a way for new people to come into the project from these partnering institutions in a positive and reaffirming way.

In this state of initiation, the collaborating team was at different stages of appreciation of Native ways of knowing and Western science and how they are similar and different. Each partner brought a different perspective to the project together with respect, knowledge, talents, skills and appreciation for the other's hard work. There were challenges in this beginning. New members may have had an awareness of the different worldviews, but not a full appreciation. But because the team held a common goal, were respectful with one another, compassionate for one another, and worked hard - ultimately the team overcame these challenges.

The Cosmic Serpent team worked hard to model collaboration with integrity. Multiple voices of leadership were heard throughout all workshops. The partners' voices were brought in and respected. It is a different type of leadership than one often sees in the Western world. Collaboration with integrity is difficult; it takes more time, it requires more money. This is something that Native people have been doing for a long, long time because it allows for work to begin in a powerful way that includes all voices and keeps the focus on the goals, the relationships, and the community for which the work is being done. Collaboration with integrity involves including the voices of all stakeholders in the development, or co-creation, of the project.

Sky City, Acoma Pueblo, NM

Building Awareness of Worldviews

Communicating across cultures can be extremely challenging and requires a commitment to openness on both sides. There has to be some preliminary protocol in place and respected by all for communication to proceed and be effective. Definition of words is essential and need to be understood by all.

For example, the word "science" has many definitions. For many Native people, science is better understood in the context of place-based knowledge, knowledge that comes through generations of experience, normally tied to the geography of the land on which the people have prehistorically and historically lived. In Native cultures, place-based knowledge is descriptive; it is often tied to specific and interrelated empirical ways of knowing. Often Native people use the word "science" in a way similar to the original Latin definition "scientia" referring to a broad definition "to know."

Native people know that when they work with scientists they have to work within the confines of scientific practices. This may often mean transferring holistic knowledge, a world of interrelationships, to a reductionistic method of thinking. This is being raised not to create a dichotomy, or to say one way is better than another, but to clarify the differences in world views and the challenges in cross cultural communication.

There is no verbatim, word-for-word translation for many terms and concepts between a verb-based Indigenous language and the noun-based English language. Indigenous languages are highly descriptive and observationally accurate.

For example, Indigenous knowledge of snow of the Yupik people in Western Alaska contains hundreds of words that describe the constantly changing snow, as affected by the constantly changing temperatures and weather. Acquisition of this extremely precise knowledge evolved through living in a harsh environment for thousands of years.

Similarly, in the Navajo language, according to Martha Jackson, Professor of Navajo Language at Diné College, "there are probably more than 200,000 ways to say 'go' in the Navajo language". This illustrates that most Indigenous languages, like Navajo, are languages of movement and process.

East: Ha'a'aah – Place of Initiation
Section 3 ... Gaining awareness of Worldviews

This juxtaposition can be an important tool to illuminate the complexity and challenges of cross-cultural communication. There are always exceptions to lists such as these. There are always variations within each worldview - each community within these large, general worldviews has their own unique story connected to their local environment. When understanding a community's worldview and the worldviews provided in this juxtaposition, we have found that it leads to positive and significant dialogue when we acknowledge that each worldview has equal value. This juxtaposition is a concrete example of what can come out of cross-cultural collaboration with integrity.

We have included this section because our Indigenous colleagues and their communities have benefited from this type of comparison. The history of colonization has created a situation in which one system of knowing was overlaid onto another system of knowing – in many cases in a forced and traumatic way. Often this led to a situation where people's traditional knowledge, culture, and language were intermingled with the mainstream colonizing culture or completely prohibited. It has been our experience that deconstructing the intermingled cultures into Indigenous and colonized worldviews has provided a seed towards understanding and respecting both worldviews on an equal basis.

Indigenous Worldviews

- Spirituality is embedded in all elements of the cosmos

- Humans have responsibility for maintaining harmonious relationship with the natural world

- Need for reciprocity between human and natural worlds - resources are viewed as gifts

- Nature is honored constantly through daily spiritual practice

- Wisdom and ethics are derived from direct experience with the natural world

Western/Eurocentric Worldview

- *"Although some kinds of culturally valued knowledge and practices (including spiritual and mystical thought) are at odds with science, a growing body of published research shows that some of the knowledge derived from varied cultures and contexts provides valid and consistent scientific interpretations."* (National Research Council, NRC, 2011, Pg 11-7).

- *"Humans depend on Earth's land, ocean, atmosphere, and biosphere for many different resources, including air, water, soil, minerals, metals, energy, plants, and animals."* (NRC, 2011, pg. 7-14)

- Natural resources are set aside for human enjoyment or available for human use/consumption.

- Spiritual practices are set apart from scientific practices

- *"Applications of natural sciences and engineering to address important global issues require knowledge from the social sciences about social systems, cultures, and economics; societal decisions about the advancement of science also require a knowledge of ethics."* (NRC, 2011, pg. 12-8)

• Universe is made up of dynamic, ever-changing natural forces	• *"There is a limited and universal set of fundamental physical interactions that underlie all known forces and hence are a root part of any causal chain, whether in natural or designed systems."* (NRC, 2011, pg. 4-4)
• Universe is viewed as a holistic, integrative system with a unifying life force	• *"Although any real system smaller than the entire universe interacts with and is dependent on other (external) systems, it is often useful to conceptually isolate a single system for study."* (NRC, 2011, pg. 4-7)
• Time is cyclical with natural cycles that sustain all life	• *"Repeating patterns in nature, or events that occur together with regularity, are clues that scientists can use to start exploring causal, or cause-and-effect, relationships."* (NRC, 2011, pg. 4-3)
• Nature will always possess unfathomable mysteries	• *"Scientists and engineers investigate and observe the world with essentially two goals: (1) to systematically describe the world and (2) to develop and test theories and explanations of how the world works."* (NRC, 2011, pg. 3-9)
• Human thought, feelings and words are inextricably bound to all other aspects of the universe	• *"Brain function involves multiple interactions between the various regions to form an integrated sense of self and the world around." "Signals that humans cannot sense directly can be detected by appropriately designed devices."* (NRC, 2011, pgs. 6-7 & 5-22)
• Human role is to participate in the orderly designs of nature	• *"The major goal of engineering is to solve problems that arise from a specific human need or desire."* (NRC, 2011, pg. 2-3)
• Respect for elders is based on their compassion and reconciliation of outer- and inner-directed knowledge	• *"Scientists need to be able to examine, review, and evaluate their own knowledge and ideas and critique those of others."* (NRC, 2011, pg. 2-3)
• Sense of empathy and kinship with other forms of life	• *"Biodiversity—the multiplicity of genes, species, and ecosystems—provides humans with renewable resources, such as foods, medicines, and clean water."* (NRC, 2011, pg. 6-19)
• View proper human relationship with nature as a continuous two-way, transactional dialogue	• *"Human beings are part of and depend on the natural world." "new technologies enable new scientific investigations, allowing scientists to probe realms and handle quantities of data previously inaccessible to them."* (NRC, 2011, pgs. 6-19 & 2-7)

We have adapted this juxtaposition of worldviews from works of Begay and Maryboy, Kawagley and Barnhardt, Knudsen and Suzuki, and a national committee made up of science education and scientific research experts for the NRC 2011. (See Section 4).

"Science and engineering—significant parts of human culture that represent some of the pinnacles of human achievement—are not only major intellectual enterprises but also can improve people's lives in fundamental ways. Although the intrinsic beauty of science and a fascination with how the world works have driven exploration and discovery for centuries, many of the challenges that face humanity now and in the future—related, for example, to the environment, energy, and health—require social, political, and economic solutions that must be informed deeply by knowledge of the underlying science and engineering." (NRC, 2011)

"And when you look at [our planet, the Earth, home, where we come from] from space, I think it is immediately clear that it is a fragile, tiny world exquisitely sensitive to the depredations of its inhabitants… All the beings on this little world are mutually dependent. It's like living in a lifeboat. We breathe the air that the Russians have breathed, and Zambians, and Tasmanians, and people all over the planet. Whatever the causes that divide us, it is clear that the Earth will be here a thousand or a million years from now. The question, the key question, the central question… is, will we?" – Carl Sagan, "The Varieties of Scientific Experience", pg. 210.

"Scientists do not seek to impose their needs and wants on Nature, but instead humbly interrogate Nature and take seriously what they find." - Carl Sagan

Magnetism: Cross-cultural presentation at our pilot workshop

"Culturally appropriate education is not just a basic human right, it is also good educational practice. The best way to contextualize education is to relate what students are learning to their cultures, communities, lives and land. While students need to learn the knowledge and skills included in tribal, state, and national standards, they and their teachers also need to respond to local concerns and have some choice in what type of learning projects they can become engaged in." (Reyhner, Gilbert, and Lockard, 2011)

"The Earth is the foundation of Indigenous peoples. It is the well of their spirituality, knowledge, languages and cultures. It is not a commodity to be bartered to maximize profit; nor should it be damaged by scientific experimentation. The Earth is their historian, the cradle of their ancestor's bones. It provides them with nourishment, medicine and comfort. It is the source of their independence; it is their Mother. They do not dominate Her, but harmonize with Her."

(Indigenous Survival International. 1991. Statement on Indigenous Peoples and conservation. Arctic Environment: Indigenous Perspectives (PPT. 41-47). Copenhagen: International Workgroup for Indigenous Affairs.)

Northwest Workshop provided a sense of place: Denali, Alaska

Proprietary Knowledge & Importance of Protocol

Federally-funded Western Science Protocol: When science is funded by the government, the knowledge gained from those studies belongs to the taxpayers and should be shared broadly. Exceptions exist with matters of national security.

Indigenous/Native Protocols: Knowledge is protected by the community and only shared with limitations and restrictions to protect its integrity, so as to avoid trivialization and marginalization of deep cultural and spiritual knowledge.

Protocol and intellectual property rights in cross-cultural informal science education are important topics and are a part of an emerging discussion and an emerging field. Protocol needs to be considered in any cross-cultural collaboration in a very careful way. All discussions of protocol and intellectual property rights stem from worldviews and notions of ownership and knowledge transmission.

In this project, even with the multi-year commitment of Cosmic Serpent Fellows and two week-long professional development workshops for each region, plus the culminating all-region conference, there was not sufficient time to delve into these emotional and challenging topics. One lesson we learned through Cosmic Serpent is the value and necessity of exploring these topics within the context of collaborating with integrity. There are now people on the cutting edge of this field of protocols and intellectual property rights (including intellectual property rights attorneys, tribal specialists, and anyone working in the field of sharing traditional cultural knowledge.) Please see this book's References Section for more information, or contact this book's authors.

Workshops showcased Indigenous ways of building and navigating using tribal protocol for knowledge.

East: Ha'a'aah – Place of Initiation
Section 4 ... Similarities with Western Science

A national committee, made up of science education and scientific research experts, worked to create the National Research Councils' publication "A Framework for K-12 Science Education: Practices, Crosscutting Concepts, and Core Ideas." (NRC, 2011) Their definition of science, as described below, is based on extensive research and knowledge and the Cosmic Serpent project agrees with this definition and is mostly congruent with the ways we described science within our project.

"Science is not just a body of knowledge that reflects current understanding of the world; it is also a set of practices used to establish, extend, and refine that knowledge. Both elements— knowledge and practice—are essential."

"In science, knowledge, based on evidence from many investigations, is integrated into highly developed and well-tested theories that can explain bodies of data and predict outcomes of further investigations. Although the practices used to develop scientific theories (as well as the form that those theories take) differ from one domain of science to another, all sciences share certain common features at the core of their inquiry-based and problem-solving approaches. Chief among these features is a commitment to data and evidence as the foundation for developing claims. The argumentation and analysis that relate evidence and theory are also essential features of science; scientists need to be able to examine, review, and evaluate their own knowledge and ideas and critique those of others. Argumentation and analysis include appraisal of data quality, modeling of theories, development of new testable questions from those models, and modification of theories and models as evidence indicates they are needed."

"Finally, science is fundamentally a social enterprise, and scientific knowledge advances through collaboration and in the context of a social system with well-developed norms. Individual scientists may do much of their work independently or they may collaborate closely with colleagues. Thus, new ideas can be the product of one mind or many working together. However, the theories, models, instruments, and methods for collecting and displaying data, as well as the norms for building arguments from evidence, are developed collectively in a vast network of scientists working together over extended periods. As they carry out their research, scientists talk frequently with their colleagues, both formally and informally. They exchange emails, engage in discussions at conferences, share research techniques and analytical procedures, and present and respond to ideas via publication in journals and books. In short, scientists constitute a community whose members work together to build a body of evidence and devise and test theories. In addition, this community and its culture exist in the larger social and economic context of their place and time, and are influenced by events, needs, and norms from outside science, as well as by the interests and desires of scientists."

The Native American paradigm is comprised of and includes ideas of constant motion and flux, existence consisting of energy waves, interrelationships, all things being animate, space/place/renewal and all things being imbued with spirit. Gary Witherspoon, studying Navajo language and art observes, "the assumptions that underlie this dualistic aspect of all being and existence is that the world is in motion, that things are constantly undergoing processes of transformation, deformation, and restoration, and that the essence of life and being is movement" (Witherspoon, 1977). The constant flux notion results in a 'spider web' network of relationships. In other worlds, everything is interrelated. If everything is interrelated, then all of creation is related. If human beings are animate ad have spirit, then "all my relations" must also be animate must also have spirit. What Native Americans refer to as "spirit" and energy waves are the same thing…

"I define science as pursuit of knowledge. The Native American mind is in constant search for meaning and reality in constant flux, not only of the Earth, but also of the cosmos. One can readily apply Einstein's definition of science as a search for reality to Native Americans. For Einstein and Western science, creation and existence were made in a certain way by God and will always remain the same; everything and anything in creation and existence just needs to be discovered by humans. Nothing is certain unless it can be referred to as a regular pattern after long-term observation. But for the Native American, even regularities are subject to change. Native Americans never claim regularities as laws, or as finalities. The only constant is change."
    –Leroy Little Bear, J.D. From the forword of "Native Science – Natural Laws of Interdependence" by Gregory Cajete, Ph.D.

The process of gaining knowledge with scientific practices is somewhat similar to gaining knowledge with Indigenous methodologies. For example, the Inupiaq in Northern Alaska use a methodology to live with the snow and ice. Over the ages, through acute observation, there have been questions and assumptions that have been tested, that show what is true about snow and ice. The language evolves with this knowledge, with testing and predictability. This process turns into knowledge to survive and is useful knowledge. It becomes embedded within the culture. We see the same thing in the Southwest, Polynesia, and among the Maya—within cultures around the world. See Aikenhead & Mitchell, 2011, and Cajete, 2011 for more information on Indigenous ways of knowing.

In both Western Science and Indigenous Knowledge, we see the use of observation, prediction, cycles, and processes, to provide understandings of nature and the universe in systems worldwide.

***"Eurocentric Science and Indigenous Knowledge represent complimentary, not separate, realities. The two can coexist."* – Aikenhead & Mitchell, 2011**

The Cosmic Serpent project brought together people from many cultures with a passion for science, Indigenous ways of knowing, and learning in informal science venues, like in the 'IMILOA 3D Planetarium, shown here.

"I have to say that my thinking about connecting and finding bridges between Indigenous knowledge and Western science never occurred to me on a museum exhibit/programming level...I have seen that there are many opportunities to interpret the connections between Indigenous knowledge and Western science and look forward to working on future programming."

—Cosmic Serpent Fellow, evaluation comment, Southwest regional network

Astronomers from two different worldviews model collaboration with integrity at a Northwest workshop by honoring each other's voice equally.

*Note that the quotes throughout this book attributed to 'Cosmic Serpent Fellow' are from the project's evaluation findings. Each quote indicates the regional workshop the Fellow attended. Quotes that were provided to the project directly are attributed to each person by name.

"As a Native Person I still have a lot of questions about Western Science and where it is taking us. At the same time I am more aware of the areas that Indigenous knowledge and Western knowledge (science) can overlap and knowledge can be shared, in some cases!"
—Cosmic Serpent Fellow, evaluation comment, California regional network

Portable Planetarium provides space for cross-cultural collaboration in astronomy.

South: Shádi'ááh – Place of Organization & Growth
Section 5 ... Building Relationships

> *Bridge People hold knowledge of both Indigenous ways of knowing and Western Science, acknowledge the integrity of both systems, and are recognized as exemplary leaders by both Indigenous communities and Western scientists. They move within both paradigms, helping to create connections.*

In keeping with Native paradigms, building relationships has been a cornerstone of Cosmic Serpent. As mentioned in the *Introduction: Igniting the Spark* section, the core relationship of the project was developed between the Indigenous Education Institute and the University of California, Berkeley's Center for Science Education. The trust, respect, and openness that developed among project partners were possible because of ample face-to-face time, frequent communication, time to connect socially and personally (not just professionally), and a strong commitment to the collaborative process. For the Cosmic Serpent Fellows, this meant experiencing multiple, intensive in-person gatherings (two workshops per region and a culminating conference); and providing opportunities for discussions, social interactions, and field trip experiences, to learn from the land. In order to create authentic, sustainable partnerships around Western science and Native ways of knowing, one needs to invest adequate time in building short and long term relationships to support this work, and to spend reasonable time face-to-face to learn from one another.

The project has continued to incorporate "bridge people" – who come to Cosmic Serpent with knowledge of both Indigenous ways of knowing and Western Science – as participants, to share their knowledge as "equals" with the museum participants. In addition to holding knowledge of two ways of knowing, bridge people are acknowledged to be exemplary leaders by both Indigenous communities and Western scientists. The bridge people have been invaluable in being able to walk and talk in both worlds, and helped to create connections and understanding among all Cosmic Serpent Fellows.

Collaborating with the NMAI (National Museum of the American Indian) was important in our building relationships. NMAI provided guidance, through Pam Woodis, at all the workshops. The Director of Education at NMAI, Claire Cuddy, came to the Pilot and Culminating conference. Two other museum educators from NMAI came to the Cosmic Serpent workshops. Pam Woodis, as a Native American, provided a strong Indigenous perspective together with Shelly Valdez, Native Pathways. The project has also provided connections between Cosmic Serpent Fellows and NMAI that have allowed for visits and discussions about future collaborations with NMAI.

The collaboration with the ASTC (Association of Science and Technology Centers) provided an important partnership. Laura Huerta-Migus, from ASTC, provided scientific perspective and was also able to understand and support the Indigenous perspective. She was a strong bridge person from ASTC. If there were things that needed to be said or covered from one perspective, she was able to provide the necessary facilitation in a respectful way for both sides. She encouraged the team and Cosmic Serpent Fellows to be participants at the ASTC conferences and to be a part of the ASTC publications. On a long-term basis, these trusting and respectful relationships allowed us to build on the Cosmic Serpent work in subsequent projects and gave us a voice at meetings outside of Cosmic Serpent events. Our partnership with ASTC, provided links between ASTC's CAISE (Center for Advancement of Informal Science Education) and the Cosmic Serpent project since some CAISE Fellows also became Cosmic Serpent Fellows.

Building relationships to collaborate with integrity - Group Photo, Taos, New Mexico

South: Shádi'ááh – Place of Organization & Growth
Section 6 ... Developing the Process

This quadrant of the Diné Cosmic Model, the south circle, is a process that goes through organization and reorganization based on experiences and evaluation. This cosmic model, the whole model, works in circles as a fractal matrix with interaction taking place at the same time. Each year, the Cosmic Serpent team would gather for a strategic planning meeting to build on existing experience and evaluation results and to plan for the coming year. In addition to this yearly planning, the Cosmic Serpent project spent weeks organizing each workshop - determining the process, the speakers, the agenda.

During and after each workshop there was an evaluation. With each evaluation and the team's view on the experience, the project would respond to this feedback, this formative feedback. The project learned that there should be fewer presentations by the Principal Investigators (team leaders) and Cosmic Serpent team - that we should allow peers to interact with one another more. So this became a part of all the following workshops. We learned that the place where we held the workshops was incredibly important - for it would dictate the interactions and reflections of the participants and the team. When there was strong connection to nature, to the land where the workshops were hosted, the participants were grateful for those connections, and more open for interaction with other participants and for more reflection on the process.

The Cosmic Serpent team saw its own growth having a direct impact on how the team approached the workshops. It took a lot of time for all the team members to understand each other. Learning how to communicate was incredibly important: how to talk and how to listen. After this growth, the team felt like it knew what it was doing and found a rhythm. This change in the team's ability to work together changed the whole spirit of the project from that point on. The team built on this spirit and it appeared to shift things for our participants - the team noticed a difference in the reception of the participants to the ideas and saw the participants become open to the growth and partnership that we tried to model.

At times, the project relied on not only the team's expertise, but also the expertise of bridge people, like Dr. Lynn Morgan, a Ph.D. in Educational Psychology. She responded to concerns that were raised, and addressed some of the feelings that people had, by using tools like "multiple intelligences" exercises and communication techniques that she brought to the project.

The model we used was fluid and flexible, so we were able to work with changes, challenges, and dynamics of the process. At the leadership level, we worked to balance the professional with the human connection. The entire Cosmic Serpent team felt that the organization of the project around the Diné Cosmic Model, with multiple workshops and time for participants to reflect and process their own experiences, helped these realizations to occur.

"I have seen this model work similarly to a scientific model. It is a general model that is adopted and applied differently in different contexts but has the same overall process in each application."

—Laura Peticolas

Northwest Follow-up Workshop field-trip to the Museum of the North, Fairbanks, Alaska

"We are opening a new, major gallery...I loved the way one of the teachers at the College spoke about plants: nutritionally, medicinally, and spiritually/culturally; and we are discussing how to incorporate these ideas into our biology exhibits."

—Cosmic Serpent Fellow, evaluation comment, Northwest regional network

Site of Northwest Workshop field-trip, the newly-opened Hibulb Cultural Center & Natural History Preserve, Tulalip, Washington

South: Shádi'ááh – Place of Organization & Growth
Section 7 ... Pilot Workshop

The Pilot Workshop took place on April 20-24, 2008 in Santa Fe, NM at the Bishop's Lodge, adjacent to traditional Tesuque Pueblo land. The setting was chosen to be conducive to reflection and partnership building: a sheltered and intimate environment with few distractions and easy access to the outdoors for breaks and fresh air. The tables included art supplies, and participants were given a small journal in which they recorded their reflections. The general components of the pilot workshop (as listed below) became the main components to each of the following workshops, with different emphases and ways of implementing the components as experience and evaluation guided the project.

Opening: The project followed traditional Native protocol, beginning with a welcome from representatives of local tribes (Laguna Pueblo, Santa Clara Pueblo, Jicarilla Apache, and Navajo) - including prayer, traditional hoop dance, and a keynote presentation on Indigenous ways of knowing.

Introductions: Everyone in the room was given a chance to introduce themselves, partially modeling Indigenous protocol and partially modeling Western protocol. This time allowed people to share their heritage and lineage in addition to their professional credentials. This style of introduction has the potential of cultivating the capacity for listening and learning from each other cross-culturally.

Plenary Speakers: A mixture of Western and Native scholars gave presentations on diverse paradigms of learning, with examples from learning experiences at the nearby Chaco Canyon National Historical Park, and juxtaposing research protocols. Two culminating presentations focused on collaboration between Western and Native astronomers highlighting the development of a digital planetarium show, and identification of commonalities between Native and Western imagery focused on science. Plenary presentations were rounded out by a discussion and response period and small group reflection.

Share-a-thon: Participants were given the opportunity to present and share their work conducted at their home institutions, in the context of bridging Indigenous and Western science, and sharing resources and handouts. This strategy facilitated continuous interaction among participants, and led to collaborations among museums as the project moved forward.

"The workshop showed me that there is a great gap between the way that the Western science world views Indigenous knowledge. This concept is going to be a long process to try to build the trust between both sides."

—Cosmic Serpent Fellow, evaluation comment, Northwest regional network

Participatory Activities: An "open lab" was set up for experiential activities related to the magnetic field as an example of a fascinating natural phenomenon that stimulated discussion on diverse ways of knowing. Participants used all their senses to create an "invisible sculpture," tracing a dipole magnetic field in 3D with a gimbaled compass. A historian of science discussed how in Western science process, a holistic approach has been used often, contrasting Michael Faraday's intuitive approach to understanding the magnetic field vs. James Clerk Maxwell's mathematical approach. Participants also witnessed a Starlab (inflatable portable planetarium) presentation given by Navajo Astronomers from Indigenous Education Institute and joined by a cultural specialist from the Navajo Nation Museum - presenting Navajo star knowledge from a Navajo perspective.

Small Group Discussion: Participants sat at round tables and worked in small groups to react to specific topics and to share their reflections on the learning that took place. This format was conducive to sharing in a safe and respectful environment that also facilitated evaluation.

Field Trip: Participants were given a chance to learn from the land, by spending a full day at Bandelier National Monument – ancestral home of the Pueblo people. The field trip fostered contemplation, reflection, and careful observation of the environment and opened a portal to the ways Native people learn. The context for the field trip and Native ways of learning was given by a Native scholar before the field trip. Representatives of the Acoma and Laguna Pueblos gave additional context on the history of the land and the site. They also focused on protocol and learning about the natural world from an integrative or holistic perspective.

Reflection and Evaluation: Every day, participants were given a chance to reflect on their own learning, and on the diverse paradigms of knowledge. The evaluation team combined mainstream and Indigenous evaluation methodologies, giving participants a chance to reflect at their own pace.

Participatory activities happened at each Cosmic Serpent professional development workshop.

South: Shádi'ááh – Place of Organization & Growth
Section 8 ... Restructure Workshops

A post pilot workshop debriefing among project team members resulted in the following lessons learned and ideas for refining future workshops.

- Meet and work with local Native people whose heritage is from the land where the workshop will take place. Allow a sufficient period of time to understand and implement the most appropriate protocols. This is essential for creating a learning environment where everyone feels comfortable.

- Native ways of learning require a focused state of being, and it can be difficult to transition from busy schedules into a reflective process that engages the whole person. It is particularly important for the core project team. It would be ideal for the team needs to gather together to convene a day ahead of the workshop, not only to take care of the logistical details, but also to "become of one mind" regarding the experience of the workshop.

- Offer an optional pre-workshop telecon with all participants to begin to introduce project and roles; offer participants the opportunity to have a one-on-one phone call with project leads.

- Placing learning about science paradigms in a broad cultural context helped set the stage for greater understanding (art, artifacts, prayers and traditional welcome, field trip, experiential activities, music and dance).

- It is important for evaluation of the project to allow participants to reflectat their own pace, instead of scheduling a daily time for reflection. The group conversation with evaluators on the last day worked well.

- PowerPoint format, in and of itself, falls short of conveying the richness of Native ways of learning. Combine presentation style with other modalities for learning. Spontaneous exchanges between Native and Western scholars and follow-up discussions were appreciated.

- Provide more opportunities to learn outdoors.

- Model introductions so they are brief and respectful.

- Provide more information on the purpose of the project and goals, role of participants and evaluation, earlier during the workshop.

- Complement Western and Indigenous presentations with hands-on activities wherever possible.

- The field trip provided a positive experience learning from the land Having Native speakers (Acoma and Laguna Pueblo) introduce their ancestral site was very effective, and made the visit authentic and accommodating. Small group discussion as an aftermath to Bandelier was very timely.

- Consider four full days plus Sunday reception to decompress schedule, if budget allows.

- Include more case studies of examples of museum applications that bridge Western and Native science, for example, the Yupik exhibit in the Anchorage museum.

- Tap expertise of participants for next workshop.

- Have the participants themselves identify overlaps or divergence of the two paradigms.

- Have more small group project oriented time, envisioning how participants might implement new learning into their work.

- Closure is very important. We implemented good pacing for ending, give-away, recognitions, and Native prayers were all appropriate and welcome.

Inspiring locations provided personal connections with nature

West: I'i'aah ~ Process of Activation ~ Living It...
Section 9 ... Southwest Workshops

Over the course of the four-year Cosmic Serpent project, we held a number of regional workshops.

"The workshop was terrifically enlightening and broadening for me. I was exposed for the first time, in depth, to Indigenous ways of knowing and knowledge; and had some of these ways demonstrated to me. It was the discussion of the knowledge itself, how the knowledge is gained and the deep history of this, and (how) it is actually employed that made my experience so rich."
—Cosmic Serpent Fellow, evaluation comment, Southwest regional network

Southwest Workshop Highlights
Spring 2009

The first full Southwest Workshop was held in Santa Fe, NM in the spring of 2009. We held most of our meetings at the IAIA (Institute of American Indian Arts) in South Santa Fe, an inspiring location where many distinguished Native American artists have been educated and trained. We learned how many Indigenous artists see their work as highly interconnected with the natural forces of a relational universe and how they gather and work with their materials in a way that promotes sustainable ecology. In addition to the workshop sessions at IAIA, we had a site visit to Poeh Museum, the tribal museum of Pojoaque Pueblo. Here we experienced break-out sessions on basket and pottery making by renowned artists—including Roxanne Swentzell—who talked about their art and the science that could be understood in the plants and soils that are used to form the baskets, statues and pots.

Touring the museum was a highlight for many participants as they experienced how Indigenous people tell their own story—in their own words with their own images—which is very different from most non-Indian museums. We visited the Planetarium at the New Mexico Museum of Natural History in Albuquerque where we viewed a Navajo star show,

Navajo weaving and Ethnobotany

and participated in hands-on activities related to Maya math and science. The following day, we had a guided tour of Sky City, at Acoma Pueblo, visiting a site that has been continuously occupied for over a thousand years. Shelly Valdez, one of our evaluators, hosted us at Laguna Pueblo, where we were privileged to view ceremonial dances, dine in family homes and visit with the Governor in his home. We also visited the tribal council chambers and heard from tribal officials.

We had a representative from the Maya community of Palenque, Mexico, Alonso Mendez, who presented with Isabel Hawkins from the Exploratorium on Maya math, using sticks and beans. Alonso demonstrated how to measure physical and solar alignments on the IAIA campus. There were many other presentations and activities, too numerous to mention here, but in all events and during every day, there were discussions of how one could find science in Indigenous culture and arts, and in observation-based Indigenous research, and also of how Western science practices could infuse and support Indigenous museums.

"Personally, in each workshop, I learn more about Indigenous knowledge and reflect on my own understanding of what science is and why we do science."

—Cosmic Serpent Fellow, evaluation comment, Southwest regional network

"Weaving has been around for hundreds of years in the southwest region. The main concept behind the curriculum is to teach simple weaving techniques with affordable materials. Materials would be cardboard looms and various types of yarns. The curriculum uses odd and even numbers to teach plain tapestry weave. Two colors of yarn are also used to create different patterns. Another section on ethnobotany could be applied on weaving. The following plants are used for dyes and soap: Navajo tea used for drinking and also as a dye for yarns. Rabbitbrush, another plant used for a plant dye. Narrowleaf yucca, its roots are used as a soap to wash wool. The chemical compound is saponin, which is a well-known lathering substance."

—Joyce Begay-Foss; Session: Navajo Weaving and Ethnobotany

West: I'i'aah – Process of Activation – Living It...
Section 9 ... Southwest Workshops

The Science of Clay

"Face to face collaboration is not something you can substitute."

—Cosmic Serpent Fellow, evaluation comment, Southwest regional network

Southwest Follow-Up Workshop Highlights
Spring 2010

The first Follow-Up Workshop took place in April, 2010. We met in Taos, NM for three and a half days. This follow-up workshop brought together Cosmic Serpent Fellows who had attended the first Southwest Workshop in Santa Fe, with the addition of several participants who were new to Cosmic Serpent.

This workshop emphasized interactive sessions and time for CS Fellows to network together; since the first Cosmic Serpent workshop, many of the museums had already initiated working partnerships between science centers and tribal and community museums. There was an afternoon visit to Taos Pueblo and outdoor sessions featuring Hawaiian navigation and Pueblo (Zuni) explanations of the Golden Mean, as well as other geometric features of ancestral Pueblo structures, such as those found in Chaco Canyon.

The concept of multiple intelligences, presented by Dr. Lynn Morgan, Board Member of the Indigneous Education Institute, was interwoven with Native perspectives throughout the workshop as a way to encourage learning in museum settings. One outcome was the creation of plans for interactive museum exhibits featuring Western and Indigenous perspectives around such themes as moccasins, trees, astronomy, ecology and baskets.

Based on positive participant feedback, break-out sessions were structured consecutively instead of concurrently so that all could attend. This workshop's sessions included chemical properties of clay, taught by Jesus Martinez of Sandia Labs. There was also an Indigenous perspective on pottery, taught by renowned Pueblo potter Clarence Cruz while he was actually creating a pot. Joyce Begay-Foss gave presentations on Navajo rug dyes which addressed plant chemistry as well as the Navajo perspective on creating dyes from plants. She also spoke about the science underlying the making of Navajo blue mush from corn and juniper ash. Over the several days, participants were enthused by these sessions and made use of their time together to network with different museums in programming and building exhibits.

West: I'i'aah – Process of Activation – Living It...
Section 10 ... Northwest Workshops

Northwest Workshop Highlights
Summer 2009

For this Northwest Workshop, we recruited museum personnel from science centers, tribal museums, and cultural museums located primarily in Oregon, Washington, and Alaska. This five day workshop was near Blaine, Washington and at Northwest Indian College, near Bellingham, WA. The workshop was opened by Swinomish elders and cultural specialists Joe McCoy and Larry Campbell, of La Connor, WA.

In this workshop, we began with traditional Indigenous introductions and continued with panel discussions to deepen our understanding of the archetype of the cosmic serpent and explored examples of possible workshop outcomes in museum settings. We discussed Indigenous ways of knowing and their differences and similarities to Western science. Break-out sessions deepened participants' knowledge of the two ways of knowing the universe. Some break-out sessions focused on experiencing Western science, presented by Oregon Museum of Science and Industry (OMSI) personnel Vicki Coats, Kyrie Kellett, Brett Kiser, and Lori Erikson. Other sessions went more deeply into Indigenous ways of knowing through direct observation and relational thinking.

Ann Riordan highlighted aspects of the creation of the Alaskan museum exhibit on Yupik survival implements, "Yuungnaqpiallerput (The Way We Genuinely Live): Masterworks of Yup'ik Science and Survival."

We spent one day at Northwest Indian College (NWIC), on the Lummi Nation, near Bellingham, where we were welcomed by President Cheryl Crazy Bull. We were grateful to Susan Given-Seymour for all her organization to make our experience so memorable. Roger Fernandes, Lower Elwha tribe, began the sessions with a talk, *Science in an Oral Tradition*. Subsequent sessions included Salish Weaving and Ethnobotanical Trails, a popular workshop presented by Theresa Parker of the Makah Museum. Theresa presented a hands-on activity on how to

"I think the people that were collected for this workshop are an amazing group of people with very similar values, but very diverse backgrounds. This made the workshop even more influential by representing many different backgrounds for various organizations and cultures, but all were willing to share and collaborate." —Cosmic Serpent Fellow, evaluation comment, Northwest regional network

Kinesthetic science education: learning about the aurora

make cedar bark bracelets, along with the ethnobotany of the cedar tree. Valerie Seacrest from NWIC taught us about Native foods gathered from Traditional lands and how they are still gathered today. Vanessa Cooper, also from NWIC, demonstrated the blending of Traditional medicine with Western medicine and gave a presentation on how to make a healing salve. Dr. Terry Maresca, an Indigenous physician, addressed the topic of combining Traditional and Western medicine in her practice at Snoqualmie Family Practice.

At the end of the day, NWIC put on a Traditional dinner. We were treated to Traditional dances by an Aleut group of young Traditional dancers (NW Unangax Culture, Snagagim Axasniikangin) from Alaska.

During the workshop, we visited the Hibulb Cultural Center on the Tulalip Reservation. We were privileged to hear from elder and traditional knowledge holder, Hank Gobin, who was directing construction of the new cultural center. We also visited the Pacific Science Center in Seattle, where we were greeted by Director of Education, Heather Gibbons, and spent several hours touring the museum, including the amazing hall of butterflies.

Traditional elder Dr. Lloyd Pinkham, Yakama Nation, and Thomas Morning Owl, Umatilla Confederated Tribes, spoke and sang to us about informal traditional science, the importance of Indigenous languages, and living one's culture. Dr. Pinkham conducted a cultural session at the ocean's edge, which was very moving for those who attended.

Additional break-out sessions featured local, Traditional foods and how they impact our health, presented by Charlene Krise, Director of the Squaxin Island Museum, and another popular session was led by Joel Halvorson and Jim Rock from Minnesota, who did an astronomy presentation in their digital portable planetarium. Ruth Ludwin, a geologist from the University of Washington, presented her ground-breaking research on earthquakes, tsunamis and landslides as discovered through Northwest Native Tradition and rock art.

There were opportunities for reflection during walks in nature. Relationships were deepened among participants, educators and the Cosmic Serpent team. As in previous workshops, participants agreed that a good foundation had been laid for collaborative partnerships and future networking.

Northwest Workshop: sharing knowledge through traditional Native Protocol of the River People.

West: I'i'aah ~ Process of Activation ~ Living It...
Section 10 ... Northwest Workshops

Northwest Follow-Up Workshop Highlights
Fall 2010

We had a spectacular Workshop Follow-Up in Fairbanks, Alaska for the Northwest Follow-up Workshop. It was wonderful to see so many familiar faces and a few new ones as well. We were happy that our NSF (National Science Foundation) Program Officer, Sylvia James, was able to join us for the week and to experience first hand how our project was going. Christopher Teren and Traci Walter from San Juan Island, WA, also joined us as professional photographers and technical support.

Robert Charlie, a renowned Athabaskan Elder, and Director of CHEI (Culture and Heritage Education Institute), opened the workshop with a greeting and welcome to Fairbanks. He and his wife Bernadette Charlie contributed immeasurably to the workshop, even hosting a potluck dinner at the conclusion of our sessions.

We continued with a group welcome from the Cosmic Serpent Leadership Team, Nancy Maryboy, Laura Peticolas and David Begay. Jill Stein reported evaluation findings from the previous Northwest Workshop, held in Blaine, WA, and how they informed the following workshops. Almost everyone had asked for more time to collaborate and network, both of which we incorporated into this Alaskan workshop.

Because relationship-building is at the heart of our project, we allowed extensive time for in-depth introductions. This gave previous Cosmic Serpent Fellows a chance to catch up on each other's experiences and accomplishments in the past year, as well as for newcomers to the group to introduce themselves and learn about the other CS Fellows.

Laura Huerta-Migus provided a dynamic presentation on the Association of Science and Technology Centers' focus on diversity, entitled "Science Centers: Awareness of Diversity." This provided a solid foundation for the work of the week.

Nancy Maryboy introduced Ray Barnhardt, Professor at the University of Alaska, Fairbanks, who spoke on the "Alaska Experience: Examples from the NSF Rural Systemic Initiative." His work was conducted through a years-long partnership with Oscar Angayuqaq Kawagley. During the week, Ray was able to join us for much of the workshop. He brought over several books that he and Oscar had co-authored and made them available for participants.

We had several presentations from different museum participants, on the topic of *"Models for Museum Outreach – Climate Change in the Northwest"* (Survival of Fish Through Land and Water Stewardship). Kyrie Kellett and Lori Erickson discussed the "OMSI Salmon

Camp: Educating the Next Generation." Jenny Atkinson, Director of the Whale Museum in Friday Harbor, WA, talked about the status of the southern resident community of Orcas in the Salish Sea. Libby Nelson gave a presentation on Tulalip Tribal Stewardship, "From the Mountain to the Sea." Robert Charlie spoke on Alaska sustainable fishing practices.

Following the talks, the project leadership team offered an Armchair Dialogue – an informal discussion on Western science and Indigenous ways of knowing that was required of all new Cosmic Serpent participants. This was a very popular session at this workshop, and continued be so at all our subsequent workshops, with many Cosmic Serpent Fellows from previous workshops joining the engaging discussion.

At times throughout the workshop, we connected to the local nature. Late at night, the opportunity to view the Northern Lights drew many of us outside to see the dancing lights in the sky. Biologist Traci Walter identified a Great Horned Owl on the roof of a nearby building. She and Christopher Teren took many photos, actually thousands, which he later stitched together into a moving picture that revealed even more aspects of the aurora than we had seen with our naked eyes.

On the second day, Paul Coleman, our favorite barefoot Astrophysicist from Honolulu, gave his famous stereotype-busting presentation. Beginning with standing on a table with a plastic bag on his head, he proceeded to break down stereotypes of Western scientists and paint a picture of the value of diversity. A lively discussion followed his presentation.

Our second presentation of the day was a Showcase of Collaborations, led by Isabel Hawkins, of the San Francisco Exploratorium, and Laura Huerta-Migus. This featured posters and informal discussions of various projects that focused on collaborations between Traditional knowledge holders and scientists. It was clear to see that multiple collaborations are taking place, and many are being seeded by the Cosmic Serpent experience.

We had an interactive roundtable discussion based on science center interactions with local communities, "Working with the Indigenous Community: Collaboration with Integrity." The roundtable was moderated by Laura Huerta-Migus. Contributors to the discussion included David Begay, Nancy Maryboy, Roxanne Gould, Jim Rock, Isabel Hawkins, Paul Coleman, Ray Barnhardt, and Kalepa Baybayan.

The second day's talks ended with Dennis Martinez giving a presentation on "Restoring the Earth's Balance: How Climate Change is Upsetting the Relationship of Earth, Fire, Water, and Air, and Indigenous Adaptation Responses." Dennis weaves local knowledge into each of his presentations, engaging the participants in a most deep and relevant manner.

Quite late at night, participants drove out to Poker Flats for a tour of the Aurora research facility and Aurora viewing. Hans Nielsen gave a

Native Hawaiian astrophysicist: Breathing new life into science

West: I'i'aah – Process of Activation – Living It…
Section 10 … Northwest Workshops

talk on the science of the Northern Lights, and his former student Laura Peticolas explained how she had done her doctoral research in this very facility.

On Wednesday, Lynn Morgan led a day-long workshop on multiple intelligences and their application to the learning experience of museum visitors can be used to reach diverse audiences. As we have seen in our other workshops, the small groups that worked together to develop prototype projects also created innovative museum exhibits that supported both Native and non-Native ways to perceive relevant content. Lynn was introduced by Nancy Maryboy and David Begay. She was assisted by Laura Huerta-Migus and Pam Woodis.

Later we visited the Museum of the North, on the University of Alaska Fairbanks (UAF) campus, and the Morris Thompson Cultural and Visitors' Center. These visits were much appreciated by the participants.

As a part of this workshop, we learned that the state of Alaska allows for hunting of an "educational moose." This is a special permit provided to Native Alaskans to hunt moose off season when it is for educational purposes. Robert Charlie, Athabascan Elder, was able to secure such a permit and the moose(!) to educate the Cosmic Serpent Fellows about the traditional knowledge that is a part of hunting and preparing a moose in Alaska. During the day, several participants went to the North Pole (a town near Fairbanks) home of Robert and Bernie Charlie to help butcher the educational moose for the potlatch dinner. People who were lucky enough to be there will long remember the day. The photos of Native Hawaiians, carrying huge chunks of moose out from the garage to cut up with a chain saw are some of the most memorable photos of the entire week.

The Northwest workshop ended with a celebratory feast. The Charlies brought moose and salmon. A friend of Lynn Morgan—Beth Bergerone, from the Geophysics Department at UAF, who does research in Antarctica—brought caribou meat. Robert Charlie led the group in Traditional Athabaskan dances with much humor and skillful drumming. In the tradition of gifting, as is usual at a potlatch, gifts were exchanged and collaborations were facilitated.

The last day, time was devoted to several discussions, all focusing on the question "where do we go from here?" Meanwhile, participants

A Cosmic Serpent Fellow modeled an 'educational moose' in red clay.

continued to work on the art pieces they were developing at their tables. We have learned that working hands-on with clay, colored pencils, and other media enables participants to concentrate more closely on issues at hand. Jill Stein of ILI (Institute for Learning Innovation) led an Evaluation Focus Group in exercises designed to learn how participants experienced the workshop.

That concluded our memorable week. We were very pleased that Sylvia James had been able to experience the interactions and collaborations that occurred between Traditional Knowledge holders and Western scientists.

"(We are) developing the new interpretive plan for our permanent exhibits: I'm meeting with the director of my museum to discuss ways to approach, first, the development of meaningful relationships with local Tribal people so we can more effectively use their words, stories, and science to help our visitors care for the planet and its interrelated components—including each other." —Cosmic Serpent Fellow, evaluation comment, Northwest regional network

Science of Cedar: Weaving Traditional cedar bracelets.

West: I'i'aah ~ Process of Activation ~ Living It...
Section 11 ... California Workshops

California Workshop Highlights
Winter 2010

The first California Workshop was held in Lakeside, CA. Participants came from throughout California, and several from Hawaii, most of whom represented the 'Imiloa Astronomy Center in Hilo. The workshop was hosted by the Barona Culture Center and Museum.

As in previous workshops, we divided our time among a variety of discussion methods. We had informal armchair and panel discussions, roundtable discussions and break-out sessions on Western science and Native ways of knowing. At this workshop, participants learned about Indigenous Navigation, Hawaiian wayfaring, Navajo and Hawaiian Astronomy, Southern California tribes' basket making and Maya math. We had one day at Balboa Park in San Diego, where participants visited various museums. We had several sessions at the Reuben Fleet Science Center which featured interactive science activities, including Navajo and Native Hawaiian astronomy, that took place in a portable planetarium with a SkySkan digital projector. The days together offered multiple opportunities to develop relationships between Western science museums, community collection-based museums, and tribal museums.

Cosmic Serpent Fellows indicated that meeting new colleagues with shared visions was a positive impact of the professional development workshops.

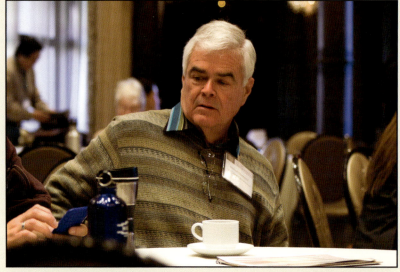

We have a new online exhibition that is a direct result of Dawn and I being part of the Cosmic Serpent team. Check it out http://www.accmuseum.org/Introduction2. The exhibition is appropriately entitled "Western Science Seeks Cultural Knowledge."
　　—Michael Hammond, Agua Caliente Cultural Museum

"The Barona tribe has been very interested in Cosmic Serpent, and the idea that the project is hoping to assist scientists in a better understanding of the Native way of knowledge, especially by inviting them to see their museum and listen to the tribe's knowledge holders. They have supported the museum's participation permitting me, their museum director, to participate as a founding Cosmic Serpent Fellow from the inaugural meeting in Santa Fe in 2008 to the Culminating Conference in Taos, 2011. The Barona Tribe and Museum hosted the California conference February 2009 on the Reservation. In 2010 in Portland, I presented on the Cosmic Serpent Program with Nancy Maryboy, Laura Peticolas, and Vicki Coats for the Western Museums Association Annual meeting."

"Science has a place in the tribal museum but only when it complements the tribal story. The tribal museum is a place where traditional knowledge supersedes any scientific explanation. It is the story of the people from their knowledge base. And in this presentation, we are very concerned with the self-esteem of tribal children and respect for the knowledge base and history of their elders."

—Cheryl Hinton, Barona Museum

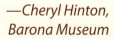

"The more I participate, the more I am realizing how little I know, how complex these issues are, and more than anything, humbling."
—Cosmic Serpent Fellow, evaluation comment

West: I'i'aah – Process of Activation – Living It...
Section 11 ... California Workshops

California Follow-Up Workshop Highlights
Winter 2011

The Cosmic Serpent California Follow-up Workshop was held in Palm Springs with the support of the Agua Caliente Cultural Museum.

The workshop began with a welcome to the land, a local tribal greeting by traditional Bird Singers from the Agua Caliente and Rincon Band of Luiseno Indians. Sean Milanovich, Cultural Specialist from Agua Caliente, began with an explanation of what we were going to hear, and he was joined by lead singer Joe Saubel, Chase Welman and Tim Siva. It was great to hear young Native singers carrying on ancient traditions and their songs set the tone for the entire workshop, one of respect and integrity for the different ways of knowing.

In this workshop, we continued our tradition of comprehensive introductions at each of the round tables, followed by a variety of talks. The first keynote speaker was Dennis Martinez from the Indigenous Peoples' Restoration Network. His illuminating talk, *Taking Care of the Land: Ecocultural Restoration, Kincentric Ecology, and Ecosystem-based Adaptation to Climate Change*, focused on issues of interest in Southern California

Angela Hardin (Federated Indians of Graton Rancheria) and Chuck Striplen (Amah Mutsun Tribal Band) then gave a multi-media presentation on *Acorn Mush*. While watching the large screen presentation of elders making acorn mush, participants listened to Angela as she gave her presentation in her traditional Coast Miwok language, using the many implements she had brought with her.

The workshop continued with a presentation by Chuck Striplen, Associate Environmental Scientist with the San Francisco Estuary Institute, *Deepening Partnerships Through Cosmic Serpent: Telling the Story of Valley Oaks in the San Francisco Bay Area: Past, Present and Future – a Public, Private and Tribal Collaboration*.

A second keynote speaker, Dr. VerlieAnn Malina-Wright, Chairman of the Native Hawaiian Educational Council and former President of NIEA (National Indian Education Association), as well as being a Board Member of IEI, gave a compelling presentation on *Indigenous Science as Sovereign Science*, using many vivid examples from her Hawaiian homeland.

West: I'i'aah – Process of Activation – Living It...
Section 11 ... California Workshops

Isabel Hawkins and Dona Maria Avila, Maya elder and knowledge holder from the Yucatan, Mexico, gave an informative hands-on demonstration on *Cooking with Corn – the Science of Corn*, bringing together Western science knowledge of corn with traditional Mayan ways of knowing and living with corn. The presentation was done in Spanish and English and enhanced with demonstrations of cooking implements and Mayan textiles.

To conclude a long and interesting day, we held one of our armchair dialogues on Western science and Indigenous ways of knowing, led by Nancy Maryboy, David Begay, Laura Peticolas, and Isabel Hawkins. This was an opportunity for Cosmic Serpent Fellows to hear and discuss issues from multiple perspectives. Ben Aleck from the Pyramid Lake Museum and Donna Cossette from the Churchill County Museum led the discussion. Ken Phillips from the California Science Center and Kalepa Baybayan from the 'Imiloa Astronomy Center contributed their perspectives to the dialogue.

Kaimana Barcarse from 'Aha Punana Leo on the Big Island of Hawaii began our sessions on Wednesday with a beautiful chant that he had written in Hawaiian especially for Cosmic Serpent. We have featured this chant at the beginning of this book.

Margaret Matthewson of Oregon State University presented an up-close and hands-on session *Landscape Maintenance for Basketry Plants with a Demonstration of Willow Splitting for Fine Weaving Strands*. This was informal science learning at its best as Margaret talked about the biology of willows and everyone got to try to split willow branches with their teeth. Experienced basketmakers, like Donna Cossette, were the best at the splitting and they helped everyone who needed assistance. After a good discussion of the content of the morning session, Cosmic Serpent Fellows participated in a Showcase of Collaborations. This enabled everyone to see how different museums were carrying out the principles of the Cosmic Serpent, bringing tenets of Indigenous ways of knowing into the science museums and using Western science in tribal museums.

Participants walked to the Agua Caliente Cultural Museum where they were graciously welcomed by Director Michael Hammond and his staff. The museum welcomed Cosmic Serpent Fellows with a reception and toured us through their new exhibit on California baskets.

Thursday sessions began with Lynn Morgan's visual presentation of *Multiple Ways of Knowing: Applying Diverse Ways of Knowing to Museum Settings, Reaching Diverse Audiences*. This interactive workshop continued most of the day. Lynn was assisted by Laura Huerta-Migus from ASTC and Pam Woodis from NMAI (National Museum of the American Indian). After learning about multiple ways of knowing, each group at a small table developed a museum exhibit using diverse way of knowing. Topics included climate change, baskets, water, and birds. The presentations of each group were extremely creative!

The final day there was a group discussion *Where Do We Go From Here?* The discussion, led by the Cosmic Serpent leadership team, focused on next steps and on the Culminating Conference which was to be held in Taos, NM in May. Additionally, the group discussed the *Generations of Knowledge* project, which OMSI had just received from the National Science Foundation. Partners collaborating in the project include the Indigenous Education Institute, Tamástslikt Cultural Institute in Pendleton, OR, and the Hibulb Cultural Center and Natural History Preserve in Tulalip, WA. Additional partners include NMAI and ILI.

These are all relationships that grew out of the Cosmic Serpent workshop. Many science centers, natural history museums and tribal museums at the workshop showed great interest in hosting this traveling exhibit when it is completed. The exhibit will focus on the value of multiple perspectives of seeing the world, in terms of sustainable ways of living in this world.

Angela Hardin and Chuck Striplen teaching the Palm Springs group how to make traditional Acorn Mush.

West: I'i'aah ~ Process of Activation ~ Living It...
Section 12 ... Culminating Conference

**Cosmic Serpent Culminating Conference
Spring 2011**

The Culminating Conference for the Cosmic Serpent project was held in Taos, NM. Eighty participants and Cosmic Serpent fellows attended from all three Cosmic Serpent regions (Southwest, Northwest, and California/Hawaii). They came from science centers, science and natural history museums, tribal/cultural museums, and tribal communities. The converging of the three regions was an opportunity for people to deepen regional connections and even establish inter-regional relationships. The conference emphasized interactive and networking sessions across all three regions on such topics as programming and exhibit development.

The Culminating Conference was opened by Benito Concha, Office of the War Chief, Taos Pueblo, who gave a warm welcome to the gathering.

For the final conference, participants submitted proposals for consideration, resulting in many excellent presentations, including the following:

- Dr Eric Jolly, Director of the Science Museum of Minnesota – *Weaving Our Worlds Together* - **Keynote**

- Chad Kalepa Baybayan, `Imiloa Astronomy Center of Hawaii, and Kaimana Barcarse, `Aha Punana Leo, Hawaii – *He Lani Ko Luna, A sky Above; A Navigation Starter*

- Richard Bugbee, Advocates for Indigenous California Language Survival, and L. Frank Manriquez, The Cultural Conservancy – *Language Connection to Indigenous Understanding*

- Dr. VerliAnn Malina-Wright, Pacific American Foundation, Indigenous Education Institute, *Sustainment: Laws of Mother Earth*, **Keynote**

- Joe Taluagon and Rex St. Onge Guadeloupe Cultural Arts and Education Center – *The Arboglyph, Star Wheel and the Shadow of the Sun*

- Melissa Nelson, San Francisco State University & The Cultural Conservancy, L. Frank Manriquez, The Cultural Conservancy, Deana Dartt-Newton, University of Washington - Burke Museum, Kaimana Barcarse, 'Aha Pūnana Leo, Richard Bugbee, Kumeyaay Community College, and Isabel Hawkins, Exploratorium – *Tiats, Tomols and Wakas: The Revitalization of Indigenous Watercraft Traditions Around the Pacific*

- Stephen Pompea, National Optical Astronomy Observatory, Kenneth Phillips, California Science Center, Laurel Ladwig, Tucana Productions, and Amy Grochowski, Maxwell Museum of Anthropology – *Connecting the Dots: Astronomy Connecting Cultures and People*

- Dr. Marvin Bolt, Adler Planetarium – *Cultures of Knowledge: Science and Society, Yesterday and Today* – **Keynote**

- Dennis Martinez, Indigenous Peoples' Restoration Network – *Indigenous Peoples as Alternative Modernities: Reclaiming Suppressed*

Voices and Narratives While Using TEK as a Complement to Western Science to Meet the Modern Challenge of Global Environmental Disaster in the Museum Setting – **Keynote**

- Evelyn Conley, Indigenous Education Institute, Roxanne Gould, Science Museum of Minnesota, Larry Campbell, Swinomish Indian Tribal Community – *Museum, Community Relationships from Tribal Perspective*

- Joyce Begay-Foss, Museum of Indian Arts and Culture – *Developing Science-based Curriculum for Navajo Weaving/Ethnobotany*

- Nancy Maryboy and David Begay, Indigenous Education Institute, and Phil Sakimoto, Notre Dame University – *GeoDome: Cross-cultural Presentation in the Planetarium*

- Jamie Powell, Denver Museum of Nature and Science and Calvin Pohawpatchoko, Jr, Atlas Institute, U of CO – *Native Science and DMNS: Integrating Indigenous Practices Through Collaborative Program Development*

- Conlin Chino, Explora! – *Learning Through Familiar Materials*

- Lindsay Irving, California Academy of Sciences, and Chuck Striplen, San Francisco Estuary Institute/Amah Mutsun Tribal Band – *Sharing World Views Through Spherical Displays: A Dome-Cast Dialogue with NOAA Partners*

- Susan Given Seymour, Northwest Indian College – *Northwest Indian College Cooperative Extension: Weaving Our Worlds*

- Linda Hogan, *Readings From the Author*

- Jim Rock and Joel Halvorson, Minnesota Planetarium Society – *GeoDome: Dakota Cultural Perspectives of the Earth and Sky*

- Arne Jin An Wong, 5D Cinergy – *GeoDome: Maya Skies*

- Dr. Willard Sakiestewa Gilbert, Northern Arizona University – *The Loololma Model: Indigenous Knowledge and Western Science Curriculum and Instruction Model* – **Keynote**

- Jill Stein, Institute for Learning Innovations, Shelly Valdez, Native Pathways, Eric Jones and Erin Johnson, Institute for Learning Innovations – – *Effective Cross-Cultural Collaborations as Seen Through Native and Western Models of Evaluation*

- Dr. Lloyd B. Pinkham, Yakama Nation – *Changes of Understanding*

- Jenny Atkinson, The Whale Museum, Cheryl Hinton, Barona Cultural Center & Museum, and Victoria Scalise, Palouse Discovery Science Center – *The Challenges, Opportunities and Strategies for Small Museums*

- Victoria Coats, Lori Erickson and Liz Rosino, Oregon Museum of Science and Industry – *The Generations of Knowledge Project*

- Heidi McCann, National Snow and Ice Data Center – *Archiving Local and Traditional Knowledge of the Arctic: Managing Data and Information in Partnership with Indigenous Communities and Earth Scientists*

- Yvonne Peterson, Skokomish Pathways Program, and Gary Peterson, The Evergreen State College – *Skokomish and Western Science*

- Michael Hammond and Dawn Wellman, Agua Caliente Cultural Museum – *The Richness of the Indian Canyons*

- Dr. Isabel Hawkins, Exploratorium, Maria O. Avila Vera, Maya Elder, and Jose Huchim Herrera, Z.A. de Uxmal, Yucatan – *Sun, Corn and the Maya Calendar*

- Chuck Striplen, San Francisco Estuary Institute/Amah Mutsun Tribal Band – *Tribal Knowledge in the Modern Resource Management Environment*

West: I'i'aah – Process of Activation – Living It...
Section 12 ... Culminating Conference

Other highlights included an evening stargazing event led by Laurel Ladwig of Tucana Productions of Albuquerque, NM, and Kalepa Baybayan. Many people enjoyed having Navajo and Hawaiian constellations pointed out, as well as looking through telescopes provided by Laurel Ladwig. There was a poster and table-top display session with over twelve very fine posters that were enjoyed by participants.

The final day of the conference, participants were honored to have a tour of Taos Pueblo led by Benito Concha. They especially enjoyed the experience of learning from the Taos point of view and wandering through the beautiful timeless pueblo.

Benito Concha, who had welcomed us, also spoke at the closing ceremony of the culminating conference, bringing closure to our Cosmic Serpent workshops. We began and ended the workshops in New Mexico, a fitting and cyclical conclusion—as well as a new beginning.

Overall, participants felt that the culminating conference was highly successful in engaging them in understanding and appreciating Indigenous way of knowing, and in building relationships towards long-term, respectful collaborations in informal learning settings. The conference also provided attendees with opportunities to become aware of and reflect on their own perceptions and beliefs around Indigenous knowledge and/or Western science, which is an important part of being able to build cross-cultural collaborative around honesty, trust, and self-awareness.

Many Cosmic Serpent fellows and participants expressed the value and benefits of the culminating conference by establishing new relationships and collaborations from other regions than their own.

Benito Concha, Taos Pueblo

"I am an Indigenous knowledge holder, so my perception hasn't changed about Indigenous knowledge, but I think that I can clearly see that my attitudes to the value of science has changed. I am more perceptive about attempting to connect science and culture, to recognize that science is culture, and to see the parallels, boundaries, and intersections."

—Cosmic Serpent Fellow, evaluation comment, California/Hawaii regional network

The following participant comments were taken from the culminating conference:

"The networking (was most valuable/beneficial). The participants were fabulous, talented, generous, open to learning."

"For myself – breaking down my stereotypes against Western science… my apologies. Since the pilot conference I have begun to incorporate 'bridging our two sciences' into my curriculum, my dissertation and life focus."

"Networking. The acknowledgement of both sciences. The interest shown by professionals in the field of science. It shows progress in the acknowledgement, giving us a future in the acknowledgement of both sciences that our society is able to tap into through museums, science centers, cultural centers, and our educational institutions."

"The culminating conference, with its welcoming and pleasant atmosphere, increased the trust, network, and openness we wanted to build. We concentrated on building both short and long-term sustainable relationship among the fellow, one that will develop and live beyond the scope of the Cosmic Serpent project."

West: I'i'aah ~ Process of Activation ~ Living It...
Section 12 ... Culminating Conference

Voices from the Workshop

"My deep experience couldn't have happened without the other participants lending their outlooks and making it a very personal exploration for us all. I was able to explore so much more deeply because this knowledge about Indigenous knowledge wasn't just being presented, it was being used and lived during the workshop. These relationships were nurtured by the very nature of the workshop, and I'm highly motivated to continue them and deepen them."

—Cosmic Serpent Fellow, Southwest regional network

"The elders and the Cultural Center have participated with us in developing an exhibit together. We met with the elders…in the museum, and we are going to redo our orientation center, and the elders have suggested that we use a phrase at the doorway there…that lets people know that the [tribe name deleted] are here, they exist. They are pleased to have that opening and the opportunity to do something, specifically from the ideas of Cosmic Serpent."

—Cosmic Serpent Fellow, Southwest regional network

"Since the workshop, I have been able to articulate (in what I hope is a relaxed and non-threatening manner) to my colleagues that there are opportunities to create a more holistic view of archeology, for example, if we include the Native ideas related to pre-history that are often presented in a separate category."

—Cosmic Serpent Fellow, Southwest regional network

"[We] have talked about a way to redo an interactive program at the museum to include the Native voice. It will just take funding. We have, however, already added two pages on this subject to a catalog of the museum that is…about to go to print."

—Cosmic Serpent Fellow, Southwest regional network

"We are making a presentation to [a] Native Nations advisory board about the ideas of Cosmic Serpent and the possibility of creating a large collaborative project with other institutions, both tribal and Western and individual Indigenous specialists. From this we will form a smaller working group to design projects that fit the ideas of Cosmic Serpent and our missions."

—Cosmic Serpent Fellow, Southwest regional network

"I put together our interpretive training for all of our volunteers at the museum, and to get the Native voice into it, we'll take all our 50 or so new volunteers for docent training out to the [tribal] Interpretive Center instead of having an anthropologist come in."

—Cosmic Serpent Fellow, Southwest regional network

West: I'i'aah ~ Process of Activation ~ Living It...
Section 12 ... Evaluation Workshops / Culminating Conference

Challenges and Successes

Having to shift from a Western notion of activation to a different way of thinking about activation was challenging. One of the ideas the Cosmic Serpent project came back to over and over again was that Indigenous knowledge is not out there for the taking, it is not for people to appropriate. Activation does not mean taking something from someone else and making it your own. For many on the team, this became the most important piece and led to the question: "How do you implement and take action in a way that's respectful and with integrity?" This was at the heart of activation and meant that there needed to be more time to figure out how to move forward with the Cosmic Serpent project. There was a progression of transition from running to implement to spending time on determining how to implement.

There were other challenges to implementation. Cosmic Serpent Fellows would come back to the team and tell of the difficulty of leaving the workshops and returning to an institution that has not been through the Cosmic Serpent project. As with all professional development projects, it was challenging to go back to work and take the learnings back in any meaningful way. This was especially true for Cosmic Serpent because of the complexity of the project. Fellows told the team that they were not exactly sure how to go back to their institution and explain the process, concepts, and relationships that they had experienced. And many came to realize that to truly implement Cosmic Serpent ideas within their institution, it was going to take more money, resources, and support than what they had at their museum.

There were implementation successes coming from the workshops. For the Cosmic Serpent team, bridge people, and several of the Cosmic Serpent Fellows, activation occurred from building on the relationships and concepts formed at the Cosmic Serpent workshops. Fellows began to invite one another and team members to their events in order to include some of the ideas of Cosmic Serpent in their events. A few Cosmic Fellows modified existing programming or exhibits to include ideas from the Cosmic Serpent workshops. Fellows and team members began to write proposals to a variety of funding agencies to help fund some of the implementation ideas. Based on feedback regarding the lack of institutional support for Cosmic Serpent ideas, the Cosmic Serpent team wrote an NSF (National Science Foundation) proposal to build on this project at three science centers. The proposal was recently funded to provide that institutional support using as a model the 'Imiloa Astronomy Center at University of Hawaii, Hilo.

North: Náhookos –
Process of transformation, renewal, and evaluation leading to sustainability.
Section 13 ... Transformation

A Native worldview of transformation does not describe a specific outcome or overarching change, but is closer to the idea of "emergent" change. While the project did not aim to create transformation from a Western sense (i.e., a complete and total change of a person), we saw many indicators of an ongoing, emergent change in Fellows' understanding, ways of thinking, and reflection on their work in bringing Indigenous knowledge and Western science together. So in this direction of the North (Náhookos), we visualize transformation as an ongoing, self-driven and emergent process that includes many steps along the way, and many possible pathways. This kind of transformation can include new realizations, deeper cultural understanding, shifts in how one thinks about his or her work, new personal and emotional awareness, and building relationships to support authentic collaboration.

Evaluation did not seek to find elements of transformation specifically, but did focus on Fellows' increased awareness and understanding around worldviews, relationship building, and ability to make changes within one's work or community as a result of their participation in Cosmic Serpent. Through the team's own experience and reflections, supported by evaluation findings, the theme of transformation emerged as an important, and perhaps essential, element in the pathway towards creating mutually respectful, cross-cultural collaborations.

New realizations

Throughout the evaluation process, many Fellows, as well as the project team members, described becoming aware of new ideas or having new realizations about worldviews, their own way of thinking, their own cultural assumptions, use of language, and cultural protocols. These moments of realization, or "aha" moments, are significant and contribute to an ongoing pathway of growth and change.

"As a Native Person I still have a lot of questions about Western science and where it is taking us. At the same time I am more aware of the areas that Indigenous knowledge and Western knowledge (science) can overlap and knowledge can be shared, in some cases." (California region)

"I can see clearly how Indigenous knowledge and Western science can work together and support a more holistic understanding of our world. I also think we can learn from Indigenous knowledge boundaries and ethics we could apply to our engagement with Western science. I feel that I can speak about Indigenous Knowledge in a more authentic way because of the great conversations and the great presentations from the workshop but I also understand it is not my role to represent this knowledge. I learned so much and was so inspired by this experience." (California region)

"Personally, each workshop I learn more about Indigenous knowledge and reflect on my own understanding of what science is and why we do science." (Southwest region)

"I wasn't aware of all the traditions with Native astronomy. Just reminding me that there are things that we (Westerners) do – things that we do that we don't intend to be biased or racist, but the decisions we make reflect that piece. Spending time in a community is really, really important because if you're on a tight deadline for a grant proposal, you still need to be respectful. It reminded me about some of those things that we do that are not intentionally disrespectful." (California region)

Deeper understanding of worldviews

Throughout the project, Fellows (mostly Western, in this case) shared how they gained a deeper understanding of Indigenous knowledge and/or Native world views, such as increased awareness and heightened sensitivity towards challenges faced by Native communities, increased understanding of how Native communities have experienced or view Western science, the importance of relationship building and trust, the importance of deep listening, and a stronger framework for thinking about Indigenous knowledge. Other areas included becoming more aware of cultural connotations of language, such as sensitivity around the use of the term "science" to describe Indigenous knowledge, and broadening perspectives beyond previously held personal biases.

"I would say that I have a better understanding of what is important to various tribes when it comes to Indigenous knowledge. It is not (just) a cultural sensitivity, but beyond the typical 'let's all just get along.'" (Northwest region)

"While I knew that there was a hesitancy to write things down held by many Indigenous people, I was not aware of the depth. This is so much clearer now. It seems to me that there is still a lot of trust building that has to be done as well as a proof period. How do you build trust without working together and seeing the results over generations? How do we develop these partnerships to build that trust if not without the facilitative help of a group like the Cosmic Serpent? My hope is that this will become clear and we will start to work on projects together and continue the conversations that started." (Northwest region)

While this learning naturally emerged mostly from the Western-oriented participants, there were certainly examples of Native participants who came to view the culture of science and scientists with more trust, especially given a long history of Western cultural domination and oppression of Native communities in the U.S. For example, one participant noted that the main value of the culminating conference was "Breaking down my stereotypes against Western science...my apologies"; and later, she adds, "I realize that it is not that Western scientists don't agree with our sciences and philosophies, they are not aware of them."

Reflective practice

Fellows shared examples of becoming more reflective practitioners, in that their learning on the project made them more aware of their own thought process and ways of approaching their work in bringing Indigenous knowledge and Western science together in informal settings. Many Fellows felt the project has made them think more deeply about their work and the complexity of cross-cultural collaboration.

"I think the idea of asking people [is important]. I know that sounds simple, but asking what people want to convey, what do they want to share? Do they want to share at all?"

"The workshop made me rethink whether science museums should try to present Indigenous knowledge if they have not been approached by Native people. I don't think we should assume that Native people want their knowledge out there for the general public to learn about. We definitely have to be very careful about how we approach this and what we choose to present." (Northwest region)

Relationship building

The theme of building relationships was strong for many Cosmic Serpent Fellows, and relationship can be seen as the foundation for all transformational change. Fellows talked about feeling that they had made deep personal connections, opened up to others, and made contacts with others that could support their work. There was a sense of growing openness and trust among participants within and across the three regions, as evidenced at the Culminating Conference.

North: Náhookos –
Process of transformation, renewal, and evaluation leading to sustainability.
Section 13 ... Transformation

"I felt like this workshop cultivated an intimate space - having created this is quite remarkable. Having created these relationships as a foundation makes the business and work come much easier. I feel comfortable contacting people and I'm genuinely interested in connecting more. I felt like we were able to establish relationships and now we have the respect and basis for accomplishing real work." (Northwest region)

"It was important for the workshop to allow for time when we could socialize and get to know each other. At first one of the activities seemed trite, yet it worked in getting the participants talking with each and sharing conclusions. There were good building blocks for future conversations (and) relationships built into the overall planning of the workshop." (Northwest region)

"Face to face collaboration is not something you can substitute." (Southwest region)

Personal and emotional learning

The Cosmic Serpent experience was a personal and emotional one for many participants. Some described learning more about themselves, their own assumptions and stereotypes through participation in the project, suggesting that what they learned had broader application to their personal lives, in addition to being relevant to their professional lives.

"I have walked or paddled great distances in both Indigenous knowledge and Western science and have expressed this as having a foot in each canoe...it's nice to know that once in a rare while both feet are in the same canoe!" (Northwest region)

"The more I participate the more I am realizing how little I know, how complex these issues are, and more than anything, humbling."

While many aspects of transformation took place throughout all stages of the project, the North created an environment to experience greater growth and transformation for Fellows and the project team. The collective experience of the Cosmic Serpent project will allow Fellows and partners involved to take this knowledge and transform their continued work and future collaborations. In the Native worldview, using the example of the spiral, there is no end in either direction in which you move within the spiral. The pathway of the spiral is continuous, allowing for emergence to transform our environments of learning; this is the pathway of the Cosmic Serpent story.

Mayan Pot by Patricia Margarita Martín Morales, from Muna, Yucatán, México.
Authentic replications of pottery of her ancestry requires knowledge of clay and pigments.

"I think the thing that is most important is the awareness within my frame of reference in all that I approach. It makes me realize that the overall museum and science paradigm needs to shift to incorporate these ideas. Yes, I met other people and yes, I encountered new ideas, but I think making sure there is something in my head that keeps popping-up, saying 'What is the tribal perspective? How does it relate to what we know in science?'"

—*Cosmic Serpent Fellow, California/Hawaii regional network*

North: Náhookos ~
Process of transformation, renewal, and evaluation leading to sustainability.
Section 13 ... Transformation

"Cosmic Serpent has changed the way I think about exhibit development. As a result of the Cosmic Serpent project, I am now looking at exhibits in a more holistic way, using a cyclical structure, and ensuring even more that all of the components are interconnected. I think about how there are connections between all the pieces and how they are related to the center, the focus. Before Cosmic Serpent, I was thinking of exhibits in a much more linear way, looking at the layout as a box with random exhibit components scattered about; the exhibit components were connected in their content, but not really in the way they flowed together spatially. Cosmic Serpent is even influencing the way we create exhibit plans and structure our exhibits in space, as well as influencing the way we convey our messages and reach our target audiences."

—Lori Erickson

The Cosmic Serpent project inspired hands-on learning like this activity at the Maxwell Museum of Anthropology in Albuquerque, NM.

North: Náhookos –
Process of transformation, renewal, and evaluation leading to sustainability.
Section 14 ... Renewal

Renewal can be interpreted in many ways. For the Cosmic Serpent project, we consider it to mean re-becoming. It does not mean starting over. It means engaging what has transpired during the past—a period of any length—and consciously becoming yourself again in a new way. In that process, there are changes that allow you sustainably to continue being you and doing what you need to do in this changing world. Within a Native worldview, renewal is similar to going through a rite of passage. An individual or group moves through a certain pathway filled with learning experiences that deepen one's ways of knowing. These experiences collectively bring new understandings that support a new level of life's continued path. It's a re-birth to the existence of place.

The culminating conference, held in May 2011, in Taos, NM, served as a key point in the renewal of the Cosmic Serpent project, bringing together Fellows from all three regional networks, along with team members, facilitators and bridge people, to connect and reconnect as one large community of practice. This was an opportunity to renew connections within one's network, build new relationships across the other regions, and to share knowledge and showcase new and pre-existing collaborative work that models the Cosmic Serpent process and themes. The gathering was well received by Fellows and infused a positive energy in the community as a whole, generating a sense of appreciation for the various pathways that Fellows had taken on the project and generating hope for future pathways and sustainability of this collaborative work.

The Cosmic Serpent Culminating Conference created an open, welcoming atmosphere in which attendees continued their personal and professional growth around what it means to work across multiple worldviews, and to collaborate with integrity and respect between science museum educators, tribal museums, and Native knowledge holders. In a project built around growing long-term and sustainable relationships, particularly in face-to-face settings, the conference served as both a culmination and a continuation of this ongoing process. At times, the conference had an atmosphere of a family reunion, with Fellows warmly greeting one another; and even those from different regions, who had not necessarily met in person, conveyed a sense of camaraderie and joint participation in a community. In this way, the culminating conference served as a way to reinvigorate and recharge attendees, some of whom are not yet finding the support systems they need in their efforts at their home institutions. For ongoing relationships and partnerships, the conference was another opportunity to build trust and connection, which will help the Cosmic Serpent community continue to grow and evolve.

The environment also played a key role in bridging and strengthening relationships. Taos, New Mexico, is considered by many to be a spiritual place that ignites a certain kind of energy. Hosting another conference at this site helped to facilitate a stronger connection to the people of Taos and, importantly, the Taos Pueblo community. Pueblo people are oftentimes closed to visitors and to sharing an intimate side of their culture. The connections made with the Taos Pueblo tribal council and having them on site for the opening and closing events solidified the continued relationship between the Cosmic Serpent family and the tribal community. To further strengthen this relationship, the council personally invited the group to visit the Pueblo, in addition to providing personal time set aside for participants to visit the Pueblo and learn from the people. This exemplified the idea of creating space to build relationship, and intimately learning from one another.

The culminating conference also supported attendees in deepening their understanding and appreciation of Indigenous ways of knowing, and hope for creating and continuing productive conversations between Indigenous knowledge holders and scientists and/or science museum educators. While attendees expressed less growth in their understanding of Western science, they did feel enabled to reflect upon their own worldviews and walked away with multiple ideas about how this experience might change their everyday practice, such as in being more sensitive to use of language, more thoughtful about how they develop programming, and more able to build long-term, respectful, collaborative partnerships.

Overall, the culminating conference invigorated and renewed the Cosmic Serpent community, helping to build connections across the three project regions, cross-pollinate ideas for project implementation, nurture ongoing relationships, and build a foundation for continued collaboration beyond the life of the grant. For this and all such projects, sustainability through continued collaboration and communication (whether online, through listservs, or in-person) will be essential for keeping the momentum and pathways moving into the future.

"It enhanced and strengthened my view that intertwining and using science and math in an Indigenous culture is very important in these days in order to help our youth and our people to straddle both worlds from an Indigenous perspective."

—Cosmic Serpent Fellow, evaluation comment,
California/Hawaii regional network

"At least one powerful connection (or re-connection) was made for me at Cosmic Serpent. I connected with staffers from (a science museum), and since that time, we've already collaborated on one proposal and have others in the works. I have a feeling that particular relationship will grow and flourish in spectacular ways."

—Cosmic Serpent Fellow, evaluation comment,
California/Hawaii regional network

Sailing with Knowledge of the Sun and Stars, Traditional Hawaiian Voyaging Canoe

North: Náhookos ~
Process of transformation, renewal, and evaluation leading to sustainability.
Section 15 ... Evaluation / Outcomes

Indigenous Evaluation

Indigenous evaluation models are not a concept that has surfaced in modern times. They are as old as the histories of the Indigenous communities themselves. Indigenous people have always had some form of "evaluation" within their societies that have perpetuated their sustainability within this world. What is different today is the use of terms and language that are now associated with the conventional approaches, tools, strategies, and methods used in today's evaluation practices. The one uniqueness surrounding Indigenous evaluation models is the weight placed on relationship. From a Native worldview, relationship is the power of place, and without relationship there is no balance. Relationship must be seen as one of the key elements of an evaluation plan. In order to create balance and continuance of valid data, the evaluators must understand and nourish the importance of their relationship to community, and to the program they are evaluating, which must begin prior to executing evaluation methodologies. In most instances, this process takes considerable time to engage in. In order to understand the cultural context of the community the evaluator is evaluating, the time given to this area is critical.

Indigenous evaluation frameworks are steeped in holistic environments. For the most part, the evaluation environments are fluid and emergent, and organically grow within and among the programs that are being served or evaluated. This type of evaluation most often times focuses on a qualitative approach that allows the evaluator to capture the story or pathway of the program being evaluated in a way that lends itself to a more culturally appropriate environment. This does not mean that quantitative methods and practices are left out of the environment; these areas are certainly an important part to conveying story.

Indigenous communities are rich with knowledge and contributions to our world as we know it; they have not always been treated as such. This is why it is important to change the historical practices of conveying negative outcomes to sharing and celebrating the successes in such a way that lend themselves to influencing continued pathways of success. Careful consideration to telling the story, focusing on positive outcomes, along with careful crafting of a mechanism for sharing the lessons learned, is essential to Indigenous evaluation frameworks.

"The Cosmic Serpent provides a unique venue for tribal Traditional knowledge keepers, Western scientists and museum professionals to gather and share their unique perspectives on scientific environmental processes in a way that honors holistic thinking and creates models for human related research questions and inquiry. The connection with museum professionals also provides an arena in which holistic thinking processes, usually only a tribal strategy, can be shared with the greater public. This educational process will lead to a new and exciting inclusive process on scientific thinking and probing of scientific questions and solutions that continues to elude the current scientific processes.

This work needs to continue, since the efforts of the Cosmic Serpent and other like-minded groups have only scratched the surface. It is an effort that is ahead of the curve in current philosophy of scientific research and I hope that the Cosmic Serpent will continue its work in educating the general public on different modes of thinking, which will bring great value in our continued existence and success as a people. It is an important part of the overall strategy to bring people together rather than divide us by leaving out crucial voices in this effort."

—Larry W. Campbell, Tribal Historic Preservation Officer, Swinomish Indian Tribal Community

"Awareness was very much increased through this participation. Especially awareness about the local nature of Native science, that it is a science of place, and that the traditions of Indigenous people of a particular place have a fundamental scientific basis. The science is observational; it is a science of experience and relationship to all living things in their local land, and also something we do not normally account for, which is a relationship with the land itself, with the mountain, the rivers, etc. It is a holistic relationship with all things. We gained awareness that humans can be deeply interconnected with everything in our planet, we need to regain that connection in the broader world."

—Isabel Hawkins

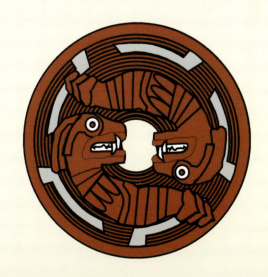

North: Náhookos ~
Process of transformation, renewal, and evaluation leading to sustainability.
Section 15 ... Evaluation / Outcomes

Collaboration Stories

Within each regional network of Cosmic Serpent are multiple stories of collaboration that have grown and evolved throughout the four years of the project and beyond. We selected one partnership per region to feature here as an example of how Cosmic Serpent Fellows used the project environment to develop deep, ongoing partnerships that bring together Indigenous knowledge and Western science in informal learning settings. Each collaboration is unique in its process and purpose, and each provides a model of collaborating with integrity across multiple worldviews. To document each collaboration story, the evaluation team followed the Dine Four Directions model and prompted Fellows during a series of phone conversations with the following questions for each goal area:

- How did this goal area play out for your collaboration?
- In what ways did the Cosmic Serpent project support this area?
- What were the challenges or lessons learned for you in this area?
- How have each of these areas played out for your institution, organization, or community?

Southwest Region
Featured Fellows:
Marie Long, Interpretive Program Manager, Arizona-Sonora Desert Museum, Tucson, AZ
Bernard Siquieros, Education Curator, Tohono O'odham Cultural Center and Museum, Topawa, AZ

Marie Long listening to Bernard Siquieros

East—*Ha'a'aah*, a place of initiation -
Practitioners will gain appreciation of a Native worldview that has commonalities with Western science

An ongoing collaboration between the ASDM (Arizona-Sonora Desert Museum) and the Tohono O'odham Cultural Center and Museum began at the first *Cosmic Serpent* Southwest Workshop (held in Santa Fe, NM, in April 2008). Bernard Siquieros, Education Curator at the Tohono O'odham Museum, and Marie Long, Interpretive Program Manager for the ASDM, had the opportunity to begin conversations during this weeklong gathering, and discovered potential pathways for collaboration between their organizations. Along with other Cosmic Serpent Fellows based in the Tucson and Phoenix areas of Arizona, they joined an informal discussion group at the workshop to strategize how they could create a local-based network of organizations with the goal of deepening collaboration across Native knowledge and Western science. Through follow-up meetings and site visits after the initial Cosmic Serpent gathering, Marie and Bernard developed multiple ways to bring together their two organizations. This primarily involved inviting elders from the Tohono O'odham Nation to consult and collaborate with the ASDM on infusing their interpretation of the Sonora Desert with local, traditional knowledge.

When asked how the Cosmic Serpent project supported their partnership at the initial phase, Marie felt that bringing together this group of professionals from the Southwest region was key: *"Going to the conference really opened the door for me; I hadn't really met any of the partners that I'm working with now. Just that alone was very important. It also made me start thinking…all of these things that we could be doing together and I had never really thought about it too much. It was really exciting to be able to start those conversations and make those connections."*

The workshop also opened up possibilities for the Tohono O'odham Cultural Center and Museum. In addition to conversations with the ASDM, Bernard noted that the workshop *"really opened my eyes to the fact that right here on the Nation we have a very scientific center in the observatory up on Kitt Peak, and how we are not fully utilizing what they have to offer. So it helped me start to think about how we need to…develop that collaborative working relationship with all of these entities. Marie was certainly very open and willing to work with us, and so this is when our working relationship began."*

Both Fellows agreed that the financial support to attend the workshops – including room, board, and transportation expenses – was also essential to the success of their own collaboration. Bernard noted that *"the fact that the Cosmic Serpent provided that financial assistance made it possible for us to go."* Marie added, *"If there weren't the funds to bring us together, I don't think it ever would have happened the way it did."*

The initial Cosmic Serpent gathering also opened up pathways for appreciating how Native and Western science might enhance and support one another. For Marie, who felt she came into the workshop with an *"awareness and appreciation of a Native worldview of science"* through extensive world travel and experience with diverse cultures, the initial Cosmic Serpent conference supported *"greater awareness of what was happening in my own backyard with Indigenous groups and their traditional ways of knowing, and getting to see all these wonderful examples of what they knew and how that really was science and complemented science."* The breadth of examples shared at the conference, including the complex science involved in Yucutan/Mayan astronomy and Native Hawaiian navigation, also helped Marie deepen her appreciation for Native worldviews and served as inspiration for her partnership with the Tohono O'odham museum and community. Another key learning for Marie was *"the whole connection of climate change and how people for centuries are so tied into nature and being connected with gathering materials for baskets or for dye-making and seeing those…seasonal changes directly related to climate change."*

For Bernard, this place of initiation created a realization of how Tohono O'odham culture and lifeways are infused with scientific understanding. He commented that before the workshop, *"I never really gave much thought to the fact that many of the things that we do as a way of our life, our culture, are actually in some ways very scientific."* Listening to some of the discussions at the workshop on science versus culture helped support these realizations. *"It kind of all made sense to me,"* Bernard shared, *"We weren't trained scientists or anything, but we understood the environment and we took that knowledge to help us in doing the things that we did. In that sense, we were basically scientists just living the way we were."*

South—*Shadiah*, a place of growth and organization
Practitioners will build relationships with museum peers, tribal community members, and people with knowledge of both Indigenous and Western science

Building on their initial introduction at the first Cosmic Serpent workshop, Bernard and Marie embarked on several specific efforts that nurtured relationship between their two communities. One important initiative involved bringing elders to the Arizona-Sonora Desert Museum to share the Tohono O'odham names, traditional uses, and cultural symbolism of plants living on the museum grounds. Bernard recalled that *"the information was respectfully taken and helped to develop a labyrinth on the grounds where people can come and enjoy the view and relax… Since the Cosmic Serpent, we've done a lot with the Arizona-Sonora Desert Museum because of initial contact at Santa Fe."* Inviting Tohono O'odham elders to the ASDM opened up many pathways and important dialogue for relationship building. Marie recounts this initial collaborative project as follows:

"We asked (the elders) what they would like the visitors to know about the Tohono O'odham people, and it was a really wonderful discussion and tour of the grounds and opportunity to capture a lot of that information… It was really timely, because right after I got back from the first conference, we were starting to discuss this new labyrinth exhibit, and that's when I stepped in and said we need to have a Native voice here to talk about this…And so it was great because our executive staff was open to that. And that's when we had everyone together — before we made any plans or anything — discussion on what should be done. It was really exciting because I felt like from the very beginning, there was that input (from elders). We received guidance on what design should be, and there was request for specific plants that should be part of the design. And there was a whole piece that Bernard and his team put together on what the man in the maze meant. And then we had the blessing of the site once it was done, which was really powerful. That would not have happened unless I had attended Cosmic Serpent. I just don't think that awareness or our connection would have been there."

Another important collaboration between the two partners was the development of the ASDM's (Arizona-Sonora Desert Museum's) Orientation Ramada, in which the Tohono O'odham elders *"spoke to the importance of water in the desert, its sacredness."* The original grant to build the orientation space focused on natural history and conservation from a Western science perspective; but the collaboration between ASDM and Tohono O'odham led to the integration of a Native voice into the interpretation of the desert. In addition, two tribal members/artists were invited to contribute art pieces to the space, including a poem and a piece of artwork depicting traditional knowledge of a rain ceremony.

An additional opportunity for building relationship between the two museums/communities includes a culture exchange in which refugee youths from all over the world (including Sudan, Iraq, Somalia and Peru) will spend a day at the Tohono O'odham Nation sharing and celebrating the diversity of cultures through games, arts, crafts, and other cultural traditions, as part of an ASDM outreach program. Bernard commented that *"people recognize the first people here; so the ASDM decided to bring them together to share each other's cultures."*

One lesson learned in this area of growth and organization was the challenge of engaging people who did not attend the Cosmic Serpent workshops. *"It is hard to articulate the experience (to others),"* Marie noted, *"but it gave us the opportunity to work together."* More support may be needed to help Cosmic Serpent Fellows translate the experience to other colleagues who did not participate in Cosmic Serpent in order to continue the growth of the model and community.

West—*li'ii'aah*, a place of activation
Museum practitioners will infuse both traditional knowledge and Western science into their programming.

Through these multiple collaborative projects that bring traditional Indigenous knowledge together with Western science perspectives, both communities have seen benefits. Bernard explains that the impacts have all been very positive: *"Our purpose here is to help people understand our history and our culture and the land. By working with the Arizona Sonora Desert Museum on these different projects, it helps us achieve that goal and it helps the visitors that come to ASDM…understand a little better about O'odham culture, O'odham views, like water… It's reflecting Tohono O'odham culture in a very positive way by being part of the Desert Museum, because it is an internationally renowned establishment."*

The ASDM has also seen broader changes as a result of partnering with the Tohono O'odham museum. In addition to integrating Native voices and perspectives into some of their interpretation and signage, practices around docent training on Native cultures have changed. While the museum used to have an anthropologist speak to docents about local Indigenous cultures, the interpretive training program has now been redesigned to involve a full-day experience at the Tohono O'odham Nation where docents experience the people, culture, and environment firsthand. Marie commented that they are *"continually educating our interpretive volunteers, because they are the ones that are articulating these stories to our guests."* In addition, Bernard or his wife, Regina, come out to talk with docents every year. *"It's a good opportunity for them to ask questions, and just to have that consistent interaction is really important. That's definitely an institutional change."*

In terms of lessons learned in this area of activation, both Cosmic Serpent Fellows agreed that the follow-up workshop, which brought everyone together again a year later (in Taos, NM), was instrumental in sustaining partnerships that began during the first workshop. Marie noted, *"It's so often I attend conferences, it's a one-time deal, you get really inspired, you go back and you start in your old patterns of working. Having that follow-up conference was really great because it brought us all back together. I think there was tremendous value in that."*

North—*Náhookos*, a place of transformation, renewal, and evaluation leading to sustainability
Practitioners and their institutions will demonstrate increased capacity to engage Native audiences in science in culturally responsive ways.

The partnership between the Tohono O'odham community and the ASDM (Arizona-Sonora Desert Museum) – which began at the initial Cosmic Serpent workshop - created pathways for deepening the integration of Native knowledge and Western science and building an ongoing and sustainable relationship between two Cosmic Serpent Fellows. During the course of the four-year project, the relationships between the two organizations deepened and resulted in numerous efforts, such as shifts in interpretive approaches, staff training, and exhibit content. Future plans include creating a Native American advisory committee at the ASDM, which would allow for ongoing, sustained input into how the museum integrates Native voices and perspectives; and including signage in the Tohono O'odham language, in addition to English. The ASDM is also involved in the newly funded NSF (National Science Foundation) project Native Universe, which will in part allow the museum to broaden and deepen its relationship with the Tohono O'odham nation.

In terms of future pathways, both Fellows felt that engaging a broader community within each of their organizations will be essential for sustaining the partnership which began through Cosmic Serpent. *"Right now it's Marie and I and sometimes (another tribal member),"* Bernard noted. *"I think we need to get more of our staff involved in this collaborative effort because we're not always going to be around… We need to get more people here thinking along those same lines so that this work will continue in all areas. Right now it's just education, but we have library and archives, and collections department, and other areas that need to come in on this. So that's something that we need to do here to create sustainability."*

Northwest Region
Featured Fellows:
Susan Sheoships, Tamástslikt Cultural Institute
Vicki Coats and Lori Erickson, Oregon Museum of Science and Industry (OMSI)

East—*Ha'a'aah*, a place of initiation
Practitioners will gain appreciation of a Native worldview that has commonalities with Western science

While the Tamástslikt Cultural Center and OMSI (Oregon Museum of Science and Industry) had connected at various levels within their museum structures, the Cosmic Serpent gatherings offered a new awareness and pathway for collaboration that has greatly deepened their individual and organizational relationships. The initial pilot workshop, held in Santa Fe, NM in April 2008, brought together members of the two museums who had not worked together before. Susan recalls, "I personally didn't have any connections (to OMSI) before Cosmic Serpent…We were aware of (OMSI's) Salmon camp, but had not participated in it." In 2008, OMSI collaborated with IEI (Indigenous Education Institute) and NMAI (National Museum of the American Indian) on a proposal for an exhibition on traditional ecological knowledge called GoK (Generations of Knowledge), which was not funded at that time. The next year, with technical and conceptual support from Cosmic Serpent, the project was reconceived in a much more collaborative way and including local tribal museum partners, Tamástslikt Cultural Center and the Hibulb Cultural Center of the Tulalip Tribes in Washington State, resulted in the team receiving funding from the National Science Foundation. They are currently co-developing the Generations of Knowledge project, which will result in a 2,000 square foot traveling exhibit (which will first show at the three partner museums), a traveling banner exhibit, and an activity kit for Native youth, along with ongoing opportunities and resources for reciprocal collaboration among the ISE (Informal Science Education) and Native American partners.

In reflecting on the collaboration, Vicki recalled that the OMSI team met Susan from Tamástslikt for the first time during the pilot workshop in Santa Fe, NM, and that having this opportunity to meet face-to-face in this context was really valuable. She recalled, *"I think that face-to-face meeting facilitated making a deeper connection, creating an opportunity to work together; and*

to explore the commonalities between Indigenous knowledge and Western science…That shared experience (of the Cosmic Serpent workshops) was helpful for us." Susan also added, *"It meant a lot for a cultural, historical museum to be on the same footing with a science museum."*

Involvement in Cosmic Serpent also led both partners to new perspectives and learning. Susan commented that her participation in two Cosmic Serpent workshops *"left a big impression. The experience colored our ideas about programming here in the museum…At Tamástslikt. We gained appreciation of the science content within our cultural/historical context and that we try to give that more validation in the way we present it to the public in exhibit planning and public program planning. We realized that has a lot of value for our audience."* For Vicki and Lori, their participation in Cosmic Serpent created a deeper awareness of Indigenous paradigms and opened the pathway for authentic, collaborative processes with Native communities in the region. Vicki shared that OMSI *"had been trying for years to figure out TEK (traditional ecological knowledge) content on our own, doing research, and we were really struggling and weren't really getting to a viable project. Then Cosmic Serpent, being able to connect with people from tribal communities and museums was so much richer and so much more authentic than reading books about TEK, trying to figure it out within, or just using resources from your own culture and your own way of knowing."* Lori indicated that OMSI's involvement in Cosmic Serpent has led to a *"greater commitment to incorporating Native knowledge in more areas of the museum."*

The deep relationships and long-term work of the Cosmic Serpent PI (Principal Investigator) Nancy Maryboy and and Co-PI David Begay were seen by the Cosmic Serpent Fellows as contributing to the success of Cosmic Serpent. Susan noted that the Cosmic Serpent gatherings and regional networks were built on decades of relationship-building by the IEI (Indigenous Education Institute) team: *"Nancy and David have so rich a history (with Native communities)… It really was a relationship-based undertaking, which has a lot to do with its success. This could not have been done as two scholars landing at the airport."* The fact that there was a follow-up workshop built into the grant was also seen as beneficial to supporting ongoing relationships and partnerships. Vicki reflected on the follow-up workshop in Fairbanks, AK (September 2010): *"By the time we did Fairbanks, the (Generations of Knowledge) project had been awarded, so it was nice to have the opportunity to meet with Susan and others we had connected with; the other big advantage of Cosmic Serpent was the other advisors and partners that became collaborators of GoK. It was nice that everyone had that relationship; it wasn't just OMSI and Tamástslikt, but IEI and NMAI and ILI, so that kind of gave everyone a feeling of knowing each other. If everyone had been new, it would have been challenging."*

South—*Shadiah*, a place of growth and organization
Practitioners will build relationships with museum peers, tribal community members, and people with knowledge of both Indigenous and Western science

Both partners agreed that the involvement of "bridge people" – which the project defined as those partners with deep grounding in both Native knowledge and Western science – were central to nurturing and sustaining the collaboration. Susan recalled that there were *"so many people who were integrators,"* providing positive models and a foundation for dialogue. As an example, Susan shared, *"We could actually witness Isabel (Hawkins) coming in as a scientist and she was so articulate about her experiences with Native TEK, that I felt we were witnessing her journey or transformation as she gained from the experience."* Vicki added that the bridge people *"were really critical to building the relationships and creating the space, the kind of experience and growth and organization that needed to happen."* Lori shared that OMSI *"could not have made Generations of Knowledge successful without their help."*

While the heart of the collaboration is about building relationship, the Fellows suggested that having a specific project to work on helped to foster this collaborative work. Vicki indicated that they may not have gotten as much out of the Cosmic Serpent experience if *"Lori and I hadn't gone to Cosmic Serpent and hadn't had Generations of Knowledge to apply it to."* She added that the *"Cosmic Serpent workshops had a huge impact on us and our understanding and practice, and with the GoK project we could carry it forward …it's easier to make progress if you're working on a common project. You still need to lay a lot of groundwork before you can do the process. Cosmic Serpent really did that for us… putting more focus on relationship than on the product."* She added, *"having to apply my Cosmic Serpent learning to GoK also really grounded it in reality. It would have been easy to think that I had attained a real understanding of TEK after the first workshop, but once I tried to apply it or explain it to other staff at OMSI, I soon discovered big gaps and really needed the ongoing workshops to deepen my understanding enough to work on GoK coherently."*

West—li'ii'aah, a place of activation
Museum practitioners will infuse both traditional knowledge and Western science into their programming.

The learning that grew out of Cosmic Serpent has manifested itself in many ways for both partners so far. Susan shared that from the education perspective, the project has helped the Tamástslikt Cultural Center emphasize science more in their exhibits and programs. She noted that the project *"has been a rich source of content for cross-curricular presentations to schools and school groups. Whatever we present, we know the outside consumer will appreciate the science content in TEK (traditional ecological knowledge). When we do interpretation, we try to incorporate scientific overlays; that's something most of our interpreters do try to do… As much as we are able to, we try to pick up interpretation of science materials in existing exhibits."* The involvement with Cosmic Serpent has also led the cultural center to *"broaden our horizon"* to feature the cultural knowledge of other Indigenous cultures. For example, they recently brought in a Mayan exhibit which focused on the scientific knowledge imbued in Mayan culture, and they also featured a film about Chaco Canyon (in New Mexico). *" We view things more regionally now,"* Susan noted. *"Our geographies have expanded and we now have a more global view."*

The Generations of Knowledge project has also been a rich ground for putting the learning of Cosmic Serpent into practice. Lori, who is serving as lead exhibit developer and co-PI of GoK from the OMSI team, shared that she is *"constantly referring to things that I learned in Cosmic Serpent for Generations of Knowledge. Really often, something will pop into my head. (Cosmic Serpent has) influenced the focus of the exhibit, and I think it will be very different than it would have been before the workshops… it's going to be much more successful in conveying the idea of traditional knowledge and Western science working together, and focusing on communities."*

For OMSI (Oregon Museum of Science and Industry), their work on Generations of Knowledge has become much more based on relationship and face-to-face interaction than it had been when they first began the project, several years before getting involved with Cosmic Serpent. Vicki noted, *"We've just done a whole bunch of trips to each of our partners to do research. I know that Lori and I were nervous about being involved, or saying the wrong thing. But having all those experiences (through Cosmic Serpent) and meeting with people from different cultures, it makes it so much easier when we go to the field. We have a much higher comfort level."* This has also led to a *"bigger picture of what's going on in your state and field,"* said Vicki. *"Now, if we happen to be traveling to eastern Oregon, we'll stop and visit (Tamástslikt), which is a nice feeling."*

North—*Náhookos*, a place of transformation, renewal, and evaluation leading to sustainability
Practitioners and their institutions will demonstrate increased capacity to engage Native audiences in science in culturally responsive ways.

Through their involvement in Cosmic Serpent and the deepening partnership to develop the Generations of Knowledge exhibit and programming, the Cosmic Serpent Fellows hope to build pathways for future work. Vicki notes that the OMSI team invited partners into Generation of Knowledge that were geographically close to the science museum's base in Portland. She commented, *"We wanted partners that were nearby, so that we had an opportunity to build the relationship. Now we are more aware of future opportunities and how we might collaborate because now we know each other, we have a shared focus in Oregon."* The fact that Cosmic Serpent was structured around a regional network was beneficial, she added, *"it did give us the opportunity to connect with a lot of people in our region that we could stay in contact with and look for other opportunities"* to collaborate. OMSI is already seeing the network of relationships starting to expand through the Generations of Knowledge project, which has helped the Cosmic Serpent Fellows begin to share their learning with other staff at their institution in a meaningful way. Vicki commented, *"What's great about Generations of Knowledge is that a lot more people are involved, so a lot more relationships are being connected; so now Liz (an OMSI evaluator), and Tim (program developer for the GoK project) have spent more time at Tamástslikt; so other people at OMSI are now getting involved with Tamástslikt."* Lori noted that OMSI is working on making other local connections with tribal communities in the urban areas as well.

Susan shared her vision for sustainability of the Cosmic Serpent project in her own education work with Tamástslikt: *"This is something that has a lot of potential. Having the opportunity to meet and listen to Native scientists…was very eye-opening as far as being aware of existing resources in Native science and reveal how much work there is to be done to expand young peoples' knowledge. As for me, it will be the next generation of museum educators to come along and activate what we learned."*

California Region
Featured Fellows:
Lindsay Irving, Production Coordinator, Visualization Studio, California Academy of Sciences
Chuck Striplen, Associate Environmental Scientist, San Francisco Estuary Institute, and Science Adviser to his tribe, the Amah Mutsun Tribal Band

East—*Ha'a'aah*, a place of initiation
Practitioners will gain appreciation of a Native worldview that has commonalities with Western science

Stemming from the first California regional workshop (held in Barona, CA, in February 2010), the California Academy of Sciences and the San Francisco Estuary Institute (SFEI) began an ongoing relationship that has resulted in a number of activities that have brought together Indigenous knowledge and Western science to develop onsite programming at the California Academy of Sciences, off-site programs, professional networks, and support of biological and cultural conservation activities. Lindsay Irving is the Production Coordinator for the Worldviews Network project (a visualization and outreach collaboration of science centers and planetariums funded by the National Oceanic and Atmospheric Administration) at the California Academy of Sciences. Chuck Striplen is an Associate Environmental Scientist at the San Francisco Estuary Institute, and is a Science Adviser to his tribe, the Amah Mutsun Tribal Band from the Monterey Bay region of the central coast of California. Chuck and Lindsay had not worked together before meeting at the initial California regional workshop for the Cosmic Serpent project in February 2010.

The initial regional workshop created an environment for building relationships and creating connections around common goals. Lindsay describes the workshop as a "catalyst" or "spark" for her subsequent collaboration with Chuck and others, which resulted in a planetarium program and live event focused on telling the story of an iconic California tree species, the Valley oak, through ecological, historical, and cultural lenses. She recalls:

"From a science center perspective, the Cosmic Serpent workshop was that catalyst for me. As a visualization practitioner at California Academy of Sciences, my job was to tell stories visually about the research that was going on in the museum here, but bringing in different perspectives was something I was interested in learning more about, and I was also interested in what were the dynamics and the work that was going on in tribal communities in this area. I always thought it was strange that the Academy never really had a formal relationship in the area or even an informal relationship that I was aware of in the eight years of working here with any specific tribal group, and yet we're a natural history museum in San Francisco. When I got there (Cosmic Serpent regional workshop), just having time at the workshop not only to hear the wonderful presentations, but to have the time to

visit and talk and build relationships with people during the conference was really fun. Chuck and I just met each other and decided to stay talking the entire week. I got to learn more about the research that his organization is doing at SFEI which is visually very rich and full of history and culture as well as science, and which I thought could support research that is going on at the Academy. Then learning about what he's doing with the tribes and with his tribe and the issues they're dealing with all over the Bay area, we just kind of put two and two together; so we said we've got all these visuals but we need help crafting these stories and also coming up with ways to engage audiences in different ways. Our work just sort of grew from there."

South—Shadiah, a place of growth and organization
Practitioners will build relationships with museum peers, tribal community members, and people with knowledge of both Indigenous and Western science

Both Cosmic Serpent Fellows felt that they were pushing the boundaries at their organizations in terms of typical approaches to projects — particularly approaches to engaging collaborators or other people outside their institutions — but that their efforts were generally supported. This institutional support helped create a pathway for the collaboration to grow. Chuck shared how this worked at SFEI: *"Coming from an institution where I have spent the past ten years trying to help change its culture, many of the staff were predisposed to thinking about traditional knowledge and Native management of natural resources going back 10,000 years, because they are very advanced environmental scientists. I've found the more advanced and nuanced a person's understanding of where society's current scientific understanding of environmental is, they tend to realize that they don't know as much as they think they do, or that there's more to the story or that there are more perspectives of the story that need to be investigated further. So, when I started talking to SFEI folks 12 years ago, I found a very welcome audience. The way that project has ended up flourishing—as directly through Cosmic Serpent and then flourishing through Cosmic Serpent- has been really appreciated by my organization and my tribe both."*

Lindsay and Chuck together developed ideas for a collaborative project right away, and found that part of the process of growth and organization for them was actually supported by attempts to quickly put their ideas into action. Lindsay recalled that shortly after the Cosmic Serpent workshop in Barona, *"I applied for a small grant to the Yahoo Employee Foundation to produce a planetarium show and live event. So (Chuck and I) said, let's bring in something concrete, let's do a show of some kind of story that would utilize the digital assets from SFEI and the digital assets of the California Academy of Sciences and blend them together in a Western science and Indigenous knowledge kind of perspective… And we said let's bring people together people at the Academy that normally would never come together—conservation organizations, policy makers, tribal groups and let's get everybody together around a theme. It was a small amount of money and we got it."* They received less funding than they requested, so they started calling foundations, including the Christensen Fund in San Francisco, whose portfolio includes biocultural conservation in the Bay area. They ended up with funding support through these organizations – one of which was the additional support to launch the "Valley Oaks" program. Lindsay noted, *"It was a lot of pavement pounding and blood, sweat and tears on the front end to really nurture the collaboration in a concrete way."*

The experience of Chuck and Lindsay is one where the directional goals of the Diné Model (initiation, growth and organization, and activation) are merged and interconnected. They sought project funding for specific projects which then increased their networks of activity to yet other tribal groups and science centers, as well as their own institutions' capacity. Chuck reflected on this period of growth and organization: *"For the Valley Oaks project, we had some key partners that included three local tribes that were involved and that were present at the final presentation – the Chair of the Michwal Wappo Tribe from Napa was there, the Chair of the Sacred Sites Committee for Graton Rancheria and their eldest Council member were there (their territory is from the Golden Gate north to the Russian River), and then my Tribal Chairman was there. There were a variety of Native folks that are affiliated with various organizations in the Bay area, Cosmic Serpent folks were there, and then a lot of local partners that are pursuing this re-oaking idea, like from the city of Napa planning commission."* Lindsay added, *"There were people there who are really engaged in putting oaks in the ground from all different sectors of society. That was great. And in our production process, we were able to bring them in and craft the narrative and the storyboard and we had a number of advisory meetings and review sessions with academics and a number of people from Chuck's network—researchers and practitioners—so it was wonderful to have them be a part of the our storymaking and the live event, which was kind of the celebration of everything we had put together."*

Cosmic Serpent supported the growth and organization of the Academy/SFEI collaboration by providing the *"intellectual environment and some of the tools to actually be able to sit down and develop these relationships."* Then, given that each partner had the knowledge, skills, and relationships in place to move to a stage of activation (in this case, creating the "Valley Oaks" planetarium project), Chuck recalls *"that then turned into something almost immediately."* In keeping with Native perspectives, the heart of the collaboration is relationship rather than the project itself. Chuck continued: *"These relationships are such that we will be turning those relationships into other manifestations of these ideas, and new ways to express some of these themes. The Valley Oaks program was just the first experiment from us having created these new relationships—coming out of the process that David Begay and Nancy Maryboy and all these folks started. We are trying to strategize, and think of other institutions in the Bay area. You know, [David and Nancy] are aware that Indian country is diverse and there are diverse scenarios and tribes with different capacities and there is not a cookie cutter approach that fits all of this. They are very aware of that we have to be very flexible and more agile and think creatively in all these different environments with different tribes and institutions where there are different levels of creativity or willingness to work outside the box. That's one of the things I really appreciate about the Indigenous Education Institute team; they are continuing to grow as they see their children grow."*

Lindsay indicated that the support of the leadership team from Cosmic Serpent was very helpful, even though she only attended the first of the three workshops (she had a baby just after the first workshop). She noted: *"In terms of the role of Cosmic Serpent in making any of these things happen, the Worldviews Network project is developing frameworks for engagement and production that are based on a number of innovative models out there and Cosmic Serpent is a major source of inspiration. Throughout our production and after the live event I was in contact with Laura, Nancy, and Chuck and we had a number of conversations over email as things came up. I got some really great feedback from them after the event as well. For example, some people would say that the presentation made them feel uneasy about how Indigenous peoples and their relationship with the land were portrayed and that they weren't sure how to think about it. Nancy let me know that this is exactly what Cosmic Serpent is for—working through these feelings. Some non-Indigenous members said 'you need to have better representation of the Native American story,' and I thought we had failed. But then Chuck and Nancy said that the whole story was infused by Native practitioners and Native people. So, if the audience can't recognize that, then maybe it's because this isn't a typical way of telling a story about Indigenous peoples…it wasn't as obvious or dramatic or romanticized as some people might expect, but it was something we felt was authentic even though it wasn't perfect."*

West—li'ii'aah, a place of activation
Museum practitioners will infuse both traditional knowledge and Western science into their programming.

Around the same time that the California regional workshops of Cosmic Serpent were taking place, a national community of planetariums and science centers, including Lindsay at the California Academy of Sciences, got together and wrote a grant to the National Oceanographic and Atmospheric Administration (NOAA) in their environmental literacy program for a project called *The Worldviews Network*, which received funding for three years. It is a collaboration of scientists, educators, artists and Indigenous groups developing best practices on how to use the digital immersive environment to bring together communities to talk about environmental change issues from a cosmic context down to a local level. Lindsay shared her thoughts about the ways in which the Cosmic Serpent project has influenced activation of the Worldviews Network:
"The Cosmic Serpent process has actually informed the ways the Worldviews Network—our planetarium network of scientists and educators and visualization people—works…The whole process that started with Cosmic Serpent has made us shift as a network and in the ways we are thinking of engaging our audiences and our communities. Instead of focusing on a big splashy planetarium show, it's more about using those visuals to build conversations and to support and nurture relationships; and that's totally from Cosmic Serpent. It's responsible for some of the lessons that we've learned in this first year and a half of this project, and so we turn to and recognize Cosmic Serpent for these things. We're about to start going through a design science process to come up with an engagement model for our future productions with different science centers across the United States. We're definitely going to be looking to our experience with Cosmic Serpent to help us draft that."

A number of other public programming efforts are underway through Lindsay's colleagues at the California Academy of Sciences. Geoffrey Willard and Eileen Harrington, also Cosmic Serpent Fellows from the Academy, have been incorporating Indigenous programming into their existing programming, including the use of talks, visits, guest speakers, cultural demonstrations, Specimen Spotlights; programs on Indigenous usage of various plant species that are part of the Academy's collections. This work was sparked for them at Barona and they have continued to do this work without requiring a lot of extra resources. Chuck has also collaborated with other Academy staff outside of his work with Lindsay, such as when he and his family built a tule boat, his culture's traditional watercraft, as part of a program and exhibit at the Academy. Chuck highlighted the complementary nature of his and Lindsay's work on capacity-building in the community with the work of the public programming personnel that is focused on building awareness and appreciation more broadly: *"That's another kind of interesting outcome that's different within the same institution, where Lindsay and Healy (the former director of the Center for Applied Biodiversity Informatics at the Academy) and the planetarium actually went the extra step to develop additional resources and develop more formal relationships with the tribes in the area. And it sounds like Geoff and Eileen are taking a more global perspective that is focused on highlighting the concepts and the ideas from Cosmic Serpent and pulling from a much broader set of cultures and communities."*

North—*Náhookos*, a place of transformation, renewal, and evaluation leading to sustainability

Practitioners and their institutions will demonstrate increased capacity to engage Native audiences in science in culturally responsive ways.

In reflecting on future directions and sustainability of the relationship which began through Cosmic Serpent, Chuck and Lindsay discussed how management issues can affect these relationships and especially active projects that require support and oversight. Focusing on the upper management level, Chuck offered, *"While I do feel we have a tremendous amount of support from certain individuals, the higher echelon of management and ownership is not always on the radar. The same could*

Opening scene of Valley Oaks program in Morrison Planetarium, December, 2011.

be said for a variety of museums and science centers—we can have good line-level relationships with people, but not always with the institutions. And that's another level of influence and education where Cosmic Serpent or Indigenous Educational Institute (IEI) as an organization can have an impact." Lindsay added that a strategy from the front-line level should also be considered, *"I'm a believer that you have to teach people by showing and to lead by doing, and the Academy has all kinds of great programs. So it's up to me and my colleagues to bring our new ideas and energies to the museum—like taking our portable planetarium and showing "Valley Oaks" to other groups off-site. This is definitely something that everybody at the Academy is supportive of."*

Both Fellows feel supported by the Cosmic Serpent network, which helps to sustain an ongoing connection to this community of shared practice. Lindsay reflected, *"I'd like to say that the newsletters are wonderful, as well as the emails that come out from the Cosmic Serpent community. It's a great community and it feels like a family or like a home where we can say that we had this shared experience. Even though I might not have met everybody, I feel like there's a foundation that I can always turn back to, to vet ideas and to experiment with, and that's exciting."* Chuck added, *"And not all networks are good at that. I'm a member of a number of networks and they're all over the board. So I focus my energy on the ones that are doing what I feel are interesting things and that are doing things to actually empower people in the network to do good things. As you can see, Cosmic Serpent is one of those."*

While the Cosmic Serpent project has completed its four-year funding period, the network which was created by the project continues to be active, and the leadership continues to be a helpful part of maintaining momentum for ongoing relationships and projects. Chuck shared this thought: *"I see all of this very much as a product of the environment that Cosmic Serpent created…At the same time, the organizing team continued to keep myself and others involved in the next iteration and evaluation. That created an atmosphere more of permanence, a movement or strategy that is working and is credible."*

"I can see clearly how Indigenous Knowledge and Western science can work together and support a more holistic understanding of our world. I also think we can learn from Indigenous Knowledge boundaries and ethics we could apply to our engagement with Western science. I feel that I can speak about Indigenous Knowledge in a more authentic way because of the great conversations and the great presentations from the workshop but I also understand it is not my role to represent this knowledge. I learned so much and was so inspired by this experience."

—Cosmic Serpent Fellow, evaluation comment, California/Hawaii regional network

Participants created many wonderful scenes during the workshops!

North: Náhookos –
Process of transformation, renewal, and evaluation leading to sustainability.
Section 16 ... Sustainability

The importance of biodiversity in the natural environment is fairly well understood and documented in the scientific world, and yet an appreciation of the importance of cultural diversity in all that we do – including science – does not seem to be as understood. In the last few workshops, it became more clear just how important it is to have that same type of (bio)diversity in scientific endeavors as we now strive for in natural ecosystems. The Cosmic Serpent workshops provided a glimpse of what could be possible if what we currently call science (Western Science in this document) embraces the principles of diversity – those same principles that have shown to allow life on Earth to thrive. What scientific knowledge will we uncover and how will it help life on Earth once we bring true diversity of thinking to science?

At the end of this project, the Cosmic Serpent team reflects on the comparison between the first workshops and the final workshops that we held. The first workshops were incredibly rewarding, but they were tough in many aspects. During these first few workshops, the Cosmic Serpent team was still forming and learning how to work together; there were participants who had come to the workshops to see what it was we were doing but who eventually decided that their work and the work of this project did not overlap; and the workshops had amazing moments of learning and opening but they were interspersed between moments of tension and closure.

By the time the Cosmic Serpent team held these final follow-up workshops in Alaska and California – the final two follow-up workshops, it had become close friends and colleagues that had the experience to support the Cosmic Serpent fellows in learning from one another. Many of the participants at these final workshops had been to prior workshops and were committed to exploring the idea of holding Western science and Indigenous knowledge with respect side-by-side; and the workshops had mostly positive and reflective moments that were truly conducive to listening and learning. Many of the Cosmic Serpent Fellows shared their voices over the past four years with the project's evaluators and team, helping the team to refine and learn how to bring such diverse and intelligent people together around the Cosmic Serpent concepts and ways of knowing.

The leads of this Cosmic Serpent project truly thank each and every person who participated in this work – for helping this project to succeed and for taking the difficult steps forward of learning from people with different ways of understanding our universe and our place in the universe.

"I think the two groups of scientists can work well together to understand the way many things have come to be and why they come to be. With open dialogue and open minds, so much can be understood and appreciated."

—*Cosmic Serpent Fellow, evaluation comment, California/Hawaii regional network*

For the future!

It is extremely important to be aware of and adhere to Indigenous intellectual property rights. This is equally true when working with non-Indigenous people. However, the concept of intellectual property rights varies considerably between the two worldviews. The deeper cultural and spiritual knowledge, in most cases, needs to remain within the tribal communities in which it is honored and lives.

Any significant cultural knowledge that a tribe wishes to share can be considered for utilization in an educational or museum setting if it is beneficial to younger generations and if it can be shared in a culturally appropriate manner, which should be determined by the Indigenous peoples themselves. It is definitely not appropriate for educational institutions or museums to unilaterally utilize cultural information as if it were their own. This is where "building relationships" becomes of vital importance, in the area of collaboration with sustainable projects.

The Cosmic Serpent project has shown that this is where Bridge People can offer valuable insights, due to their years of working with diverse populations and gaining respect from the Western and Indigenous communities. Working in areas of Indigenous intellectual property rights is highly complex and should be undertaken with the advice of cultural advisors and legal experts, whenever necessary.

In the case of federally-funded scientific projects, other procedures must be followed, and other expectations should be adhered to. Large research institutions often have written copyright policies that may include individual patents, sharing of all federally-funded data, to name a few. These have a fundamental conflict with community-based intellectual property rights. This complex subject will need to be explored in the years to come.

North: Náhookos –
Process of transformation, renewal, and evaluation leading to sustainability.
Section 16 ... Sustainability

Sustainability is at the heart of the Cosmic Serpent story, and is what will carry this story along many pathways into the future. This legacy document is part of that sustainability, in that it captures and documents the learning of Cosmic Serpent in order to inspire and guide others who embark on similar paths of cross-cultural collaboration. In this section, we share lessons learned gathered through an ongoing process evaluation that documented the project team's own learning, as well as input gathered from formative and summative evaluation efforts with Cosmic Serpent Fellows. These are the lessons learned that we hope will carry this project and others into the next cycle of the four directions, and that will continue an ongoing pathway of bringing Indigenous knowledge and Western science together by collaborating with integrity.

Lessons Learned for Future Collaborative Work

As the Cosmic Serpent project is unique in its approach to modeling the type of cross-cultural collaboration the project seeks to support, we present the key lessons learned at all levels of the project, including the leadership team, evaluation team, and the Fellows. These lessons learned are not meant as a one-size-fits-all model, nor are they necessarily prioritized over other experiences and time-tested strategies in this area of work, but rather as a means to share our own learning on the project with the larger field, and as inspiration for future ways of bringing these worldviews together.

• **Through the pathway of sharing the Cosmic Serpent story and reflections on the lessons learned, future collaborations need to be considerate of the time and space needed for creating a relationship prior to activation of program activities.** It is the heart of relationship that stimulates and shapes the pathways of genuine collaborative work. As a result of designating this as the main gateway for creating a foundation, the consideration of time, financial support and key individuals involved needs to be strategic.

• **The physical environments where the partnerships unfold are also critical to the success of these types of collaborations.** Factors that contribute to the success of the collaborative pathway include places that provide positive energies; Indigenous communities where accessibility to community is at hand; rural settings with access to significant cultural places that could be used in on-site activities; and consideration of lodging accommodations that reflect an appropriate environment.

• **The activation of activities needs to be purposeful and have meaning for the collaborators so that application of these learned experiences can happen within and around their local institutions.** With this said, the activities and presentations always need to be considerate of balance of voice. Creating environments where all voices are heard, shared and experienced will help sanction and influence more opportunities for this type of work. Sometimes there may need to be more time spent on orienting the audience to Indigenous worldviews. Consideration of where the participants are in terms of knowledge levels is recommended.

• **At the funding agency level, the considerations of the amount of time needed to activate these types of collaborations needs to

be considered in terms of funding timelines, and financial support systems. While there is an appreciation of the financial support systems from funding agencies, part of the effort to share the imbalances in this area are respectfully presented for future considerations in creating environments for future support to these types of collaborations.

- **Collaboration is filled with complexities, but is valuable and rewarding.** Each partner needs to be open and willing to engage in complexities, and in an emergent process that may not be clear at all times. An enriching environment of learning and growth is created only when each partner is open, trusting, and committed to building the collaboration. Ample time must be allotted for in-person gathering (relationship building); it is in the context of physical presence that trust can best be built, and mutual understanding and learning can take place. An annual meeting is generally not enough, rather, multiple gatherings throughout the year and at key points throughout a project.

- **Facilitating partnerships with a Native paradigm can be effective and is generally inclusive.** In environments that bring together Native and Western knowledge, it is fruitful to let the Native worldview guide the collaborative process. As a holistic, emergent approach aimed at inclusion and balance of voices, the Native paradigm naturally creates an equitable environment that allows for multiple perspectives. This approach also serves to help right the historical imbalances between Indigenous and Western paradigms by spending time immersed in Native ways of knowing. Finally, while Native partners are well aware of Western protocols, there is often a much steeper learning curve on the side of Western partners, especially those with little or no experience in Native cultures and worldviews.

- **Participants benefit from engaging with a positive, hopeful attitude, and a belief that things will work.** In terms of historical trauma of Indigenous people there is evidence that research has perpetuated harmful documentation, to the point that despair has infiltrated into community environments, resulting in unhealthy impacts. Culturally, Indigenous people used practices and concepts of celebrating experience that allowed for positive nurturing of a particular environment. With this said, it is important that activation, engagement, and sharing of story be focused on celebrating the successes of experience. Scientific research shows the more you apply the positive, the more positive outcomes surface. Indigenous communities value this concept of celebrating story and believing in positive pathways.

- **Collaboration often requires willingness to commit personal interest in the mission/goals of the project.** This type of collaboration involves a "whole person" approach, in that it is not merely an engagement in ones professional life, but a willingness to reflect on and engage with one's whole self. Partners and Fellows on the project often spoke of the personal growth they experienced, in addition to what they learned in relation to their professional work.

North: Náhookos –
Process of transformation, renewal, and evaluation leading to sustainability.
Section 16 ... Sustainability

- **Personal transformation may be needed in order to achieve project or collaborative goals.** As mentioned above, this type of collaborative process can be deeply personal, touching on deeply held beliefs and understanding of the world and our place within it. With partners entering collaborations at very different levels of understanding and experience, it is necessary to allow time for personal growth, learning and reflection, as these are essential to the success of this work. Personal transformation can happen in small, iterative steps, and is an ongoing process that will evolve over time. It is important to allow space for this to happen, and to make room for the personal and the emotional within this space.

- **This type of collaboration takes trust, respect, time, commitment, frequent communication, and many in-person visits to develop and sustain.** This is necessary and desirable for creating a truly collaborative process in which we value and give voice to all perspectives; and it supports an evaluative process that is also inclusive of many voices. The team also learned that more time was needed for not only the Fellows, but the leadership and evaluation teams as well, to spend in the two first areas of the Dine model. Because of this, impacts to the budget challenged financial balance. It is important to consider this area when the collaboration is centered on implementing Indigenous worldviews. It takes considerably more time and commitment to move through this type of environment. Similarly, budget structures must reflect a true balance of voices and input, rather than one side having significantly more support than the other. Equity and balance must be reflected at all levels of the project.

"We are working on a proposal to develop an exhibit on the relationship between IK (Indigenous Knowledge) and WS (Western Science) and the workshop not only gave us insight into ways to do this, but also provided connections between Tribal communities we can partner with for this project."

—*Cosmic Serpent Fellow, evaluation comment, Northwest regional network*

"It definitely helped me understand that the way I was raised is a very recent and specific way of seeing the world. Mostly it was an excellent and timely reminder that there are many ways of knowing that have been around for centuries."

—*Cosmic Serpent Fellow, evaluation comment, Southwest regional network*

Dennis Martinez

First, I have to say that I have learned a lot, especially astronomy—Native and Western. Albuquerque was my first experience in an observatory. Stunning! Then, there were all of the new acquaintances from many fields. And the networking that led to a presentation at the San Francisco Exploratorium and Cal State and at Palm Desert, where I linked up with still more folks. I am grateful for the opportunities I had to give presentations at the Cosmic Serpent conferences. Traveling to northern New Mexico twice, my first time in Fairbanks, Alaska, then Palm Springs, Barona, was special. Beautiful places. Reconnecting with old friends was a special treat.

Finally, all of our group discussions and presentations, I think, gave me (and probably others, especially our scientist friends) a very clear idea of what all of the Cosmic Serpent meetings were about: How we "bridge" Western and Indigenous ways of knowing. The answer for me was simply that these two stand-alone epistemologies do not need external validation but have an integrity of their own— yet, as we saw several times—there are places where they are complementary.

From a Native point of view, Western science is a powerful quantitative, more abstract tool that TEK (Traditional Ecological Knowledge) can employ to complement Indigenous qualitative, observational, place-based knowledge. Another tool in the tool-box for traditional Indigenous peoples. And what an experience we all shared in arriving at this place where Native and Western science can work together in tackling our unprecedented environmental challenges!

Baskets carry profound stories. The basket on the left was woven by Margaret Matthewson and other Cosmic Serpent Fellows during the Palm Springs workshop. In the basket, she incorporated all the voices and images of the workshop. She began the basket in Palm Springs but she did not finish it. She said that this is an unfolding and emerging story that has yet to be completed. She gave the basket to the Cosmic Serpent team for safekeeping. It is treasured and will be present to record more and more stories as time goes on.

Advisors

1. Anecita Agustinez: (Navajo), Chumash Community Liaison, CA, and Native Community Leader

2. Dan Burns: Environmental Sciences, Director EnvironmentalScience Degree at Northwest Indian College, Lummi Nation, Bellingham, WA, and former Director STEM Projects AIHEC

3. Greg Cajete PhD: (Santa Clara Pueblo), Education, and Chair, Native Studies, University of New Mexico

4. Dave Chittendon: Vice President, Education, Science Museum of Minnesota, St. Paul, MN

5. Paul Coleman PhD: (Native Hawaiian), Astrophysics, Institute for Astronomy, University of Hawaii, HI

6. Roberto Gonzalez-Plaza PhD: (Hispanic, Mapuche), Biology, NW Indian College, Lummi Nation, Bellingham, WA

7. José Huchim Herrera: Director of Archeology at Uxmal, Instituto Nacional de Antropología e Historia, Mérida, Yucatán, México

8. Angayuqaq Oscar Kawagley PhD: (Yupik), Biology, University of Alaska, and Co-Director, Alaska Rural Systemic Initiative

9. Leroy Littlebear JD: (Blackfoot), Educator, University of Lethbridge, Alberta, Canada; Former Director of Native Studies at Harvard University.

10. Becky Menlove: Director of Exhibits, Utah Museum of Natural History, Salt lake City, UT

11. Bonnie Sachatello-Sawyer PhD: Director, Hopa Mountain, Inc., Bozeman, MT

12. Dennis Schatz: Associate Executive Director, Pacific Science Center, Seattle, WA

13. Rob Semper PhD: Physics, Executive Associate Director, The Exploratorium, San Francisco, CA

14. Rose Von Thater: (Tuscarora/Cherokee), Silver Buffalo Consulting, Trans-Cultural Educator, and Founding Director, Native Science Academy, Berkeley, CA

15. Stephen Wall JD: (White Earth Chippewa), Department Chair, Indigenous Studies, Institute of American Indian Arts (IAIA), Santa Fe, NM

16. Marian Wilson-Comer PhD: Biological Sciences, Chicago State University and Executive Director, Illinois Louis Stokes Alliance for Minority Participation (IL-LSAMP), IL

Cosmic Serpent Fellows

Ben Aleck
Barbara Ando
Victoria Atkins
Jenny Atkinson
Helen Augare
Larry Banegas
Kaimana Barcarse
Raymond Barnhardt
Jennifer Bates
Kalepa Baybayan
Rose High Bear
Joyce Begay-Foss
David Belardes
Lora Boome
Angelita Borbon
Theresa Breznau
Paula Brown-Williams
Richard Bugabee
Carol Bylsma
Christopher Cable
Maria Calvi
Larry Campbell
Veletta Canouts
Robert Charlie
Bernadette Chato
Conlin Chino
Ka Chun Yu
Victoria Coats

Paul Coleman
Evelyn Conley
Kitty Connely
Laura Conner
Margie Connolly
Christine Conte
Kay Cope
Donna Cossette
Clarence Cruz
Deana Dartt-Newton
Linda Deck
Debbie DeRoma
Carol Diebel
Laurie Egan-Hedley
Jim Enote
Valerie Epaloose
Lori Erickson
Karen Evangelista
Lisa Falk
Samantha Ferguson
Roger Fernandes
Ann Fienup-Riordan
Karen Fort
Gary Fujihara
Ben Garcia
Monica Garcia
Kirby Gchachu
Heather Gibbons

Susan Given-Seymour
Jason Gobin
Roberto Gonzalez-Plaza
Roxanne Gould
Durinda Gouley
Amy Grochowski
Joel Halvorson
Michael Hammond
Julia Hansen
Terri Hansen
Kimberly Hanson
Angela Hardin
Eileen Harrington
Isabel Hawkins
Katie Hessen
Robyn Hidgon
Cheryl Hinton
Linda Hogan
Philip Hoog
Lisa Hoover
Donna House
Sarah Huschle
Lindsay Irving
Christine Janson
Jo Jenner
Arne Jin An Wong
Robert Johnson
Aolani Kailihou

Eric Kansa
Dawn Kaufmann
Kyrie Kellett
Ka'iu Kimura
Larry Kimura
Brett Kiser
Kathryn Klein
Toshi Komatsu
Charlene Krise
Laurel Ladwig
Timothy Lee
Carol Leone
Marc Levine
Matthew Lewis
Gail Loeffler
Marie Long
Ruth Ludwin
VerliAnn Malina-Wright
L. Frank Manriquez
Bradley Marshall
Dennis Martinez
Margaret Mathewson
Paulmichael Maxfield
Rich McConaghy
Joseph McCoy
Nikki Melchior
Lynn Morgan
Libby Halpin Nelsen
Melissa Nelson
Marnie Olcott
Norberto Oropez
Thomas Morning Owl
Theresa Parker
Teri Paul

Heather Paulsen
Ruth Pelz
Joyce Perry
Yvonne Peterson
Kenneth Phillips
Joyce Pinkham
Lloyd Pinkham
Stephen Pompea
Jami Powell
Andrew Puckett
Terrie Restivo
Linda Rhine
Rebecca Roadman
Jim Rock
Lynda Romero
Bonnie Sachatello-Sawyer
Alyce Sadongel
Teri Saffon
Philip Sakimoto
Mari Lyn Salvador
Cory Samia
Carmen Sandoval
Jessica Sapunar-Jursich
Victoria Scalise
Valerie Segrest
Sun Rose Iron Shell
Susan Sheopships
Bernard Siquieros
Rex St. Onge
Jim Stone
Chuck Striplen
Joe Talaugon
Lisa Thompson
Cristina Trecha

Nadine Ulibarri
Maria Avila Vera
Lisa J. Watt
Dawn Wellman
Wendy Weston
Allison Wieland
Geoff Willard
Reylynne Williams
Ted Williams
Erin Wood

Participating Institutions

'Aha Punana Leo
'Imiloa Astronomy Center of Hawaii
A:shiwi A:wan Museum and Heritage Center
Agua Caliente Cultural Museum
Aha Punana Leo, Mahele Honuakai
Anasazi Heritage Center/Crow Canyon Archaeological Center
Anchorage Museum
Arizona State Museum, University of Arizona
Arizona-Sonora Desert Museum
Association of Science-Technology Centers (ASTC)
Barona Cultural Center and Museum
Barona Reservation
Black Oak Casino
Blackfeet Community College
Blas Aguilar Adobe Museum Acjachemen Cultural Center
BLM – Anasazi Heritage Center
Bradbury Science Museum
California Academy of Sciences
California Science Center
Chabot Space and Science Center
Challenger Learning Center of Alaska
Churchill County Museum
City of Las Cruces Museum System
Confederated Tribes of the Umatilla Indian Reservation
Denver Museum of Nature and Science
Eastern Sierra Institute for Collaborative Education
Edge of the Cedars State Park Museum
Explora
Exploratorium
Federated Indians of Graton Rancheria
Forest Song Educational Services
Guadalupe Cultural Arts and Education Center
Healthcare Cost Containment United Association
Heard Museum
High Desert Museum
Hilbulb Museum and Natural History Preserve
Hopa Mountain
Huhugam Heritage Center
Huxley College of Environmental Sciences
Imaginarium Discovery Center
Imiloa Astronomy Center of Hawaii
Indigena de Desert Sonora
Indigenous Education Institute
Indigenous Peoples' Resource Network
Institute for Astronomy, University of Hawai'i
Ka Haka 'Ula O Ke'elikolani College of Hawaiian Language
Kumeyaay Community College
Las Cruces Museum of Natural History
Lawrence Hall of Science, University of California, Berkeley
Makah Cultural Research Center
Marylhurst University
Maxwell Museum of Anthropology, University of New Mexico
Maxwell Museum of Anthropology, University of New Mexico
Minnesota Planetarium Society
Museum of Indian Arts and Culture
National Museum of the American Indian

National Optical Astronomy Observatory
Navajo Nation Museum
New Mexico Museum of Natural History & Science
New Mexico Museum of Natural History Foundation
New Mexico State University
Northwest Indian College
OpenContext.org
Oregon Museum of Science and Industry
Oregon State University
Pacific American Foundation
Pacific Science Center
Palouse Discovery Science Center
Payamkawichum Kaamalam
Phoebe A. Hearst Museum of Anthropology, UC Berkeley
Poeh Cultural Center and Museum
Pyramid Lake Museum
Reuben H. Fleet Science Center
San Diego Museum of Man
San Diego Natural History Museum
San Francisco Estuary Institute
San Francisco State University and the Cultural Conservancy
Santa Ynez Cchumash Indian
Science Museum of Minnesota
Skakomish Nation
Skokomish Education Center
Skokomish Indian Tribe
Southwestern Indian Polytechnic Institute
Squaxin Museum Library and Research Center

Swinomish Indian Tribal Community
Tamástslikt Cultural Institute
The Cultural Conservancy
The Cultural Heritage and Education Institute
The Huntington Library, Art Collections, and Botanical Gardens
The Imaginarium
The Living Desert
The Museum at Warm Springs
The Museum of Contemporary Native Arts (MoCNA)
The Whale Museum
Tohono O'odham Nation Cultural Center & Museum
Tribal Museum Planners and Consultants
Tulalip Tribes Hibulb Cultural Center
Turtle Island Dignity & Education
University of Alaska- Anchorage
University of Alaska- Fairbanks
University of Alaska- Museum of the North
University of Colorado, Boulder
University of Hawaii Institute for Astronomy
University of Washington - Burke Museum
Utah Museum of Natural History
Water Resources Education Center
Water Resources Education Center
Wisdom of the Elders
Yakama Heritage Museum

Contributors

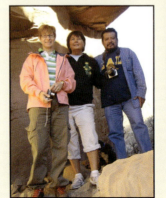

Cosmic Serpent Team Leadership

Principal Investigators:

Nancy C. Maryboy, Ph.D.
Indigenous Education Institute
Friday Harbor, WA

Co Principal Investigators:

Laura Peticolas, Ph.D.
UC Berkeley,
Berkeley, CA

David Begay, Ph.D.
Indigenous Education Institute
Santa Fe, NM

Cosmic Serpent Team

Renee Frappier
UC Berkeley
Berkeley, CA

Laura Huerta-Migus
Association of Science and Technology Centers (ASTC)
Washington, DC

Ruth Paglierani
UC Berkeley
Berkeley, CA

Ashley C. Teren
Indigenous Education Institute
Jacksonville, OR

Pam Woodis
National Museum of American Indian
Washington, DC

Cosmic Serpent Evaluators:

Jill Stein
Institute for Learning Innovation
Maryland

Shelly Valdez, Ph.D.
Native Pathways
Laguna Pueblo, NM

References and Resources

Aikenhead, G. and H. Michell. 2010. *Bridging Cultures: Indigenous and Scientific Ways of Knowing Nature.* Pearson Publishing.

Allen, S., J. Gutwill, D. L. Perry, C. Garibay, K. M. Ellenbogen, J. E. Heimlich, C. A. Reich and C. Klein. 2007. Research in museums. In J. H. Falk, L. D. Dierking and S. Foutz (eds). *In Principle, In Practice: Museums as Learning Institutions.* Lanham, MD: AltaMira Press.

Babco, E. 2005. *Report on the Status of Native Americans in Science and Engineering.* Prepared for the National Academy of Engineering Workshop on Engineering Studies at the Tribal Colleges. http://www.cpst.org/NativeIV.pdf

Barnhardt, R. and A. O. Kawagley. 2005. Indigenous Knowledge Systems and Native Ways of Knowing. *Anthropology and Education Quarterly* 36(1): 8-23. http://www.ankn.uaf.edu/Curriculum/Articles/Barnhardt-Kawagley/Indigenous_Knowledge.html

Barnhardt, R. and A.O, Kawagley. 2010. Alaska Native Knowledge Network, Center for Cross-Cultural Studies, University of Alaska, Fairbanks.

Brayboy, B. and A. E. Castagno. 2008. *How might Native Science inform "Informal Science Learning?"* National Research Council Board on Science Education.

Cajete, G. 2000. *Native Science: Natural Laws of Interdependence.* Santa Fe, NM: Clear Light Publishers. http://www.iaiancad.org/nep/courses/indig1/knowledge/readings/rr8know_Cajete.htm

Cajete, G. 2006. *Tenets of Native Philosophy.* Santa Fe, NM: Institute of Native American Indian Arts. http://www.iaiancad.org/nep/courses/indig1/knowledge/readings/rr8know_Cajete.htm

Castillo, A. R. 2009. The whizz of electrons and the wisdom of elders: Linking traditional knowledge and Western science. *Traditional Knowledge Bulletin,* July 29. http://www.ias.unu.edu/sub_page.aspx?catID=705anddddlID=963

Chinn, Pauline (2011) "Developing a Sense of Place and an Environmental Ethic: A Transformative Role for Hawaiian/Indigenous Science in Teacher Education?" J. Reyhner, W.S. Gilbert & L. Lockard (Eds.). in Honoring Our Heritage: Culturally Appropriate Approaches to Indigenous Education (pp. 75-95). Flagstaff, AZ: Northern Arizona University.

Coats, V., N. C. Maryboy, I. Hawkins, K. Baybayan, P. Woodis and L. Erickson. 2010. *Navigating Native American Knowledge and Western Science.* Presentation at the Association of Science-Technology Centers Annual Conference, Honolulu.

Cobern, W. (1994). Point: Belief, understanding, and the teaching of evolution. *Journal of Research inScience Teaching*, 31, 583–590.

References and Resources

Cooper, K. C. and N. Sandoval (eds). 2006. *Living Homes for Cultural Expressions: North AmericanNative Perspectives on Creating Community Museums.* Washington, DC: National Museum of the American Indian.

Dunlap, R. E., Van Liere, K. D., Mertig, A. G., & Jones, R. E. (2000). Measuring endorsement of the New Ecological Paradigm: A revised NEP scale. Journal of Social Issues, 56, 425- 442.Johnson, E., Kirkhart, K., Madison, A.M., Grayson, B., & Guillermo, S.F. (2008). "The Impact of Narrow Views of Scientific Rigor on Evaluation Practices for Underrepresented Groups," in N. Smith & Brandon, P., eds., *Fundamental Issues in Evaluation,* New York: The Guilford Press, pp. 219-242.

Faircloth, S. C. and J. W. Tippeconnic III. 2010. *The Dropout/Graduation Crisis Among American Indians and Alaska Native Students: Failure to Respond Places the Future of Native Peoples at Risk.* http://www.civilrightsproject.ucla.edu/research/dropouts/faircloth-tippeconnic-Nativeamerican- dropouts-2010.pdf

Friedman, A. 2009. *Framework for Evaluating the Impacts of Informal Science Education Projects.* National Science Foundation. http://www.informalscience.org/researches/EvalGuide_work.pdf

Friedman, A and R. von Thater-Braan. 2005. One Earth, One Universe: Professional Development on Native and Western Science Perspectives. WIPCE Conference Proceedings.

Hawkins, I. 2005. Introduction to space science. In N. C. Maryboy and D. Begay, *Sharing the Skies: Navajo Astronomy – A Cross-Cultural View.* Tucson, AZ: Rio Neuvo Press.

Heimlich, J. E., J. H. Falk and S. Foutz. 2009. *Free-Choice Learning and the Environment.* WalnutCreek: AltaMira Press.

Hill, Jr. R. W. 2005. In search of an indigenous voice. In *The Native Universe and Museums in theTwenty-First Century.* Washington, DC: National Museum of the American Indian.

Huerta Migus, L., N. C. Maryboy, D, Begay, L. Peticolas, J. Stein, S. Valdez and P. Woodis. 2010.*Weaving New Science paradigms: Collaborations with Native American/Hawaiian Partners.*Presentation at the Association of Science-Technology Centers Annual Conference, Honolulu.

Iaccarino, M. 2003. Western science could learn a thing or two from the way science is done in other cultures. *European Molecular Biology Reports* 4(3): 220-223. http://www.nature.com/embor/journal/v4/n3/full/embor781.html

International Institute for Sustainable Development. 2007. *Traditional Knowledge and Sustainable Development* (A. Kothari, ed.). http://www.iisd.org/pdf/2007/igsd_traditional_knowledge.pdf.

Jolly, E. J. (2002). "On the Quest for Cultural Context in Evaluation," in *The Culture Context of Educational Evaluation: A Native American Perspective,* National Science Foundation, Directorate of Education and Human Resources, Division of Research, Evaluation, and Communication (pp. 14-22).

References and Resources

Keane (2008). Science Education and Worldview, *Cult Stud of Sci Education* 3:587-621, DOI 10.1007/s11422-007-9086-5.

Kellert, S. 2005. *Building for Life: Designing and Understanding the Human-Nature Connection.* Washington, DC: Island Press.

Kothari, A. 2007. Traditional Knowledge and Sustainable Development. International Institute for Sustainable Development. http://www.iisd.org/pdf/2007/igsd_traditional_knowledge.pdf.

LaFrance, J. (2004). Culturally Competent Evaluation in Indian Country, New Directions in Evaluation, No. 102.

Lewis and Aikenhead (2001). Introduction: Shifting Perspectives from Universalism to Cross-Culturalism, *Science Education*, 85, 1-3.

Maryboy, N. C. and D. Begay 1998. *Nanit'a Sa'ah Naaghai, Nanita'a Bikeh Hozhoon, Living the Order: Dynamic Cosmic Process of Dine Cosmology.* Ph.D. Dissertation.

Maryboy, N. C. and D. Begay. 2003. *A Cosmic Planning Model for the World Hope Foundation.* Indigenous Education Institute.

References and Resources

Maryboy, N. C. and D. Begay. 2006. Finding the Thunderbird in Navajo Astronomy. In: *Viewing the Sky Through Past and Present Cultures,* Selected Papers: Oxford VII International Conferences on Archaeoastronomy.

Maryboy, N. C. and D. Begay. 2005. *Sharing the Skies: Stories and Activities of the Navajo and Western Cosmos.* Boulder, CO: World Hope Foundation.

Maryboy, N. C. and D. Begay., I. Hawkins and T. Cline. 2005. Ways of Knowing from Father Sky: Native and Western Research Protocols–From Paradox to Collaboration. *WIPCE Conference Proceedings.*

Maryboy, N. C., D. Begay, and L. Nichol. 2006. Paradox and transformation. *WINHEC Journal* (March 29).

Mazzocchi. F. 2006. Western science and traditional knowledge: Despite their variations, different forms of knowledge can learn from each other. *European Molecular Biology Reports* 7(5): 463-466. http://www.ncbi.nlm.nih.gov/pmc/articles/PMC1479546

Medin, D. 2006. Native American Identity and Learning. *Northwestern University News* (Spring). http://www.sesp.northWestern.edu/newsCenter/inquiry/?issueSelect=4andNewsID-109

National Museum of the American Indian (NMAI). 2005. *The Native Universe and Museums of the Twenty-first Century.* Washington, DC: Smithsonian Institution.

National Research Council (NRC). 2009. *Learning Science in Informal Environments: People, Places and Pursuits.* Washington, DC: National Academies Press. http://www.nap.edu/catalog.php?record_id=12190

National Research Council (NRC). 2010a. *Expanding Minority Participation: America's Science and Technology Talent at the Crossroads* (pre-publication). Washington, DC: National Academies Press. http://www.nap.edu/catalog/12984.html

National Research Council (NRC). 2011. *Committee on Conceptual Framework for the New K-12 Science Education Standards.* Washington, DC.

National Science Board (NSB). 2006. *Science and Engineering Indicators 2009.* Women, Minorities, and Persons with Disabilities in Science and Engineering. http://www.nsf.gov/statistics/wmpd

National Science Foundation (NSF). 2003. *The Cultural Context of Educational Evaluation: A Native American Perspective.* Arlington, VA: Author. http://www.nsf.gov/pubs/2003/nsf03032/nsf03032.pdf

Native Hawaiian Education Council. 2002. *Hawai'i Guidelines for Culturally Healthy and Responsive Learning Environments.* Hilo, HI: University of Hawai`i at Hilo.

Nelson-Barber, S., LaFrance, J., Trumbull, E., Aburto, S. (2005). Promoting Culturally Reliable and Valid Evaluation Practice. In Role of Culture and Cultural Context in Evaluation, pg 59-83.

North American Association for Environmental Education - NAAEE (2004). Nonformal Environmental Education Programs - Guidelines for Excellence. ISBN 1-884008-89-5

References and Resources

Olson and Loucks-Horsley (2000), Inquiry and the National Science Education Standards: A Guide for Teaching and Learning, *Editors*; Committee on the Development of an Addendum to the National Science Education Standards on Scientific Inquiry; National Research Council, ISBN-10: 0-309-06476-7

Peticolas, L. M., B. Mendez, I. Hawkins, C. Whitworth. 2008. Effective Strategies for Engaging Latino/Hispanic Audiences in Astronomy during the International Year of Astronomy. *Astronomical Society of the Pacific's Conference Series, Vol. 400,* Edited by M. G. Gibbs, J. Barnes, J. G. Manning, and B. Partridge. San Francisco: Astronomical Society of the Pacific, p.422.

Peticolas, L., N. Maryboy, D. Begay, R. Paglierani, R. Frappier and A. Teren. 2011. Lessons Learned from Cosmic Serpent, a professional development project for informal educators on science and native ways of knowing, Earth and Space Science: Making Connections in Education and Public Outreach. Edited by Joseph B. Jensen, James G. Manning, and Michael G. Gibbs. Astronomical Society of the Pacific, p.291.

Pomeroy, D. (1994). Science education and cultural diversity: Mapping the field. *Studies in Science Education*, 24, 49–73.

Reyhner, Jon, Willard Sakiestewa Gilbert, Louise Lockard, "Honoring our Heritage," Northern Arizona University Press, Flagstaff, AZ 2011

Schultz, P. W. (2002). Inclusion with nature: Understanding the psychology of human-nature interactions. In P. Schmuck, & P. W. Schultz (Eds.), *The psychology of sustainable development*. Kluwer Academic Publishers, Boston, MA.

Snively, G. and J. Corsiglia. 2001. Discovering indigenous science: Implications for science education. *Science Education* 85: 6-34. http://www.d.umn.edu/~bmunson/Courses/EdSe4255/Snively-IndigenousScience.pdf#search='indigenous%20science%20knowledge%20base

Stein, J., E. Jones and S. Valdez. 2009. *Cosmic Serpent Northwest Workshop Evaluation: Summary of Results*. Institute for Learning Innovation and Native Pathways.

Thompson, S. C. G. & Barton, M. A. (1994). Ecocentric and anthropocentric attitudes toward the environment. *Journal of Environmental Psychology, 14,* 149-157.

Quinn Patton, M. (2011). *Developmental Evaluation: Applying Complexity Concepts to Enhance Innovation and Use*. New York: The Guilford Press.

University of Colorado. 2010. Traditional Inuit Knowledge Combines With Science to Shape Arctic Weather Insights. *Press Release,* April 7. http://www.colorado.edu/news/r/4e08dcc74fc91f79f3acb5321cc50a7a.html

Valdez, S. 2004. *Reflections on Indigenous Evaluation: A Native Perspective*. Native Pathways.

Whipple, D. 2008. Breaking the ice. *Nature Reports: Climate Change* (April 24). http://www.nature.com/climate/2008/0805/full/climate.2008.38.html

Credits

Photos in this book by: Ashley C. Teren, Christopher S. Teren, Traci L. Walter, Nancy C. Maryboy, Ph.D., Isabel Hawkins, Ph.D., Chad Pearson, (IDEUM), A. Berry, (IDEUM), scientists on behalf of the general public (NASA)

Diagrams on pages 6 and 7 courtesy I.E.I. with graphics by Ashley C. Teren and Jason Gobin, Tulalip Nation, WA

Illustrations on pages 8 and 16: Jason Gobin, Tulalip Nation, WA

Painting on page 15 courtesy Ross LewAllen

Cherokee uktena (serpent) image by Joseph Erb on pages 60 and 71

Tree Photograph page 85: Tim Horn, California Academy of Sciences

Painting on page 98-99 courtesy I.E.I. painting by Melvin Bainbridge

Cover Original Image by Daniel Smith, Salish Nation, Canada

Back Cover Design / Photograph: Christopher S. Teren

All images in this book copyright protected by their perspective artists. No image in this book may be used or reproduced without explicit written permission from the copyright holder or Indigenous Education Institute.

Acknowledgments

Gratitude and Appreciation To...

Mary Marcussen, our grant writer and thinker extraordinaire, for carrying our seed of a vision toward a funded project; Sylvia James, our brilliant and supportive NSF program officer for supporting our project in unimagined ways while helping us sort through all the NSF requirements; Jim Spadaccini and his amazingly talented staff at Ideum for building our website, creating three precious slide-shows, and taking beautiful photographs at several of our workshops; Isabel Hawkins for her pioneering spirit, birth of this project and continued support of the work even after retirement; Pam Woodis and Claire Cuddy for creating a wonderful connection to the National Museum of the American Indian and voice to the tribal museums; Laura Huerta-Migus for providing an amazing ability to synthesize and facilitate the Cosmic Serpent work and to provide connections to the Association of Science and Technology Centers (ASTC); Wendy Pollock for providing our first connections to ASTC and for seeing the potential of this work; Martin Storksdieck, for creating our first connections to the Institute for Learning Innovation, for his pioneering spirit, and for contributing to this legacy document by way of the NRC 2011 Framework; the Indigenous Education Institute board for their wise words and unending support of our project through many twists and turns – many members of which attended and supported the Cosmic Serpent workshops: Evelyn Conley, Lynn Morgan, VerlieAnn Malina-Wright, Larry Campbell, and Polly Walker; our knowledgeable and wise advisors listed in this book who provided amazing presentations and voice to the project and to our workshops; to the outstanding and trusting Cosmic Serpent Fellows listed in this book for standing by the project even when they were not quite sure where it was going and for providing the heart and soul of the project; the Cosmic Serpent evaluation team for not only evaluating our program, but for providing many moments of guidance in referring to our goals and objectives and for providing another authentic model of collaboration with integrity: Jill Stein, Shelly Valdez, and Eric Jones; the University of California, Berkeley Internal Review Board for their support of maneuvering the federal laws regarding working with human subjects research and evaluation; the teams at the Indigenous Education Institute and University of California, Berkeley for providing the hard work in developing, creating, and sustaining, and creating the Cosmic Serpent project, for providing graphic and photography support, for providing spectacular logistics support for the workshops, and much, much more: Christopher Teren, Ashley Teren, Renee Frappier, Ruth Paglierani, Igor Ruderman, Karin Hauck, Darlene Yan, Leitha Thrall, Karen Meyer, Traci Walter, and Dan Zevin; Cathy Cavanagh for her support to IEI and her enthusiasm for our projects; Robert and Bernadette Charlie, for their incredible hospitality and teachings in Alaska; and last but certainly not least, we are grateful for the American Public and the National Science Foundation for funding this effort of collaboration with integrity.

THANK YOU! AHEEHEE! MAHALO! WADO! MERCI! GRACIAS! DAWA EE!

With the wisdom of two worlds, we look to the future...

Kyle Swimmer

Laguna Pueblo, Eastern Band Cherokee, Chippewa-Cree
New Mexico Institute of Mining and Technology

This material is based upon work supported by the National Science Foundation under the collaborative grants No. 0714629 and 0714631. Any opinions, findings, and conclusions or recommendations expressed in this material are those of the author(s) and do not necessarily reflect the views of the National Science Foundation.